ORDERED APR 30.93
FROM ENGLAND
JUNE 7. 1993

COST $35.
+ POST + HANDLE

Emmerdale

The First Twenty Years

Emmerdale
The First Twenty Years

Bill Hill and Michael Heatley

BOXTREE
in association with

YORKSHIRE
TELEVISION

First published 1992 by Boxtree Limited

10 9 8 7 6 5 4 3 2 1

A catalogue record for this book is available from the British Library

Editor: Edward Leeson
Design: Penny Mills
Jacket Design: Karizzma Enterprises Ltd
Picture Research: Brian Jeeves

Printed and bound in Italy by OFSA s.p.a.

BOXTREE LIMITED
Broadwall House
21 Broadwall
London SE1 9PL

ISBN 1 85283 196 0

Contents

'Emmerdale' celebrates its twentieth birthday this year and it is a pleasure to be introducing this special twentieth anniversary book as the producer of this top drama serial.

The programme has come a long way since episode one hit our screens on 16 October 1972. It first started life as a lunch-time entertainment, mainly appealing to housewives who would stop their household chores, make a cup of tea and enjoy a break in the middle of their busy day. It proved to be very popular and soon the audience was growing and a slightly later slot was found for the programme, which meant that more people could tune in. The tea-time slot allowed a wider audience to follow the ups and down of Beckindale and its inhabitants and before too long the viewing figures proved that the programme deserved an early evening slot and so it was moved, first to six thirty, and then to its current seven o' clock slot.

Over the years it has tackled many issues from Annie's tranquillizer addiction to Nick Bates as a single parent, but never has it preached to its audience. 'Emmerdale' is first and foremost an entertainment and, judging by the mailbag, that is what the audience appreciate it as.

The mix of tragedy and comedy, combined with the drama and unique rural setting, make for one of Britain's best-loved television programmes.

I first came to 'Emmerdale' in 1989 as story editor. For many years I had worked at the BBC, first as an assistant floor manager (television stage manager), and then as script editor on 'EastEnders'. When I joined the programme we had only moved into our new home in Farsley – the spinning shed of an old textile mill – very recently. The mill is still working but they no longer needed the spinning shed. In ten weeks it was transformed into a working production centre. Stuart Doughty, my predecessor, and Timothy Fee, the production supervisor, were responsible for getting everything together and settling everyone in, and it is they who set up the team which brings 'Emmerdale' to the screen.

The people who make 'Emmerdale' are a dedicated group of profes-sionals, who care passionately about the programme and work hard to make it the winner it is. This book is a fitting tribute to everyone, cast and crew alike, who over the past twenty years have worked so tirelessly.

I look forward to the future of 'Emmerdale' which goes from strength to strength. I am proud to be the producer of one of the top soaps and wish it well for the next twenty years.

Of course 'Emmerdale' wouldn't be what it is without one important group of people… the viewers.

I hope *you* enjoy this book. Do keep watching the programme – we have plenty of good stories lined up for the coming year.

MORAG BAIN

1992

Comings and Goings

The first name to be mentioned in any history of 'Emmerdale' has to be that of Kevin Laffan. Already a distinguished playwright and author with West End productions to his name, it was Kevin's evocation of a Yorkshire farming community – complete right down to the fictional names to describe the surrounding countryside – that so caught the public's imagination.

The selection of the farm and village used for filming was made by the first director of 'Emmerdale', Stuart Fleming. The same farm has been used for twenty years; and, though its identity has never officially been divulged by Yorkshire Television, it has been successfully located by hordes of sightseers.

The initial cast-members stayed relatively unchanged at first. In 1974, Jack

The original Jack Sugden, played by Andrew Burt.

Sugden went off to Rome to write the script for the film of his bestselling novel *Field of Tares*. That was the last we saw of Andrew Burt, who at the start of the screen life of 'Emmerdale' was the 'soap dish' as far as the media was concerned; but the character was later to be brought back in the equally manly shape of Clive Hornby, who plays him to this day.

By the time Jack Sugden was brushing up on his Italian phrases, 'Emmerdale' had already said goodbye to three-quarters of the Skilbeck family – first twins Sam and Sally (played by real-life twins from a Batley family) and then their mother, Peggy (played by Jo Kendall). A collision at a level crossing and a fatal aneurysm left Matt Skilbeck (Frederick Pyne) alone in the world. In real life, the programme was proving

Matt, Annie and Wilks with the Skilbeck twins at the farm in 1973.

more than just another television series, and cast-members had to decide the level of commitment they were prepared to give. The contracts then, as now, were annual affairs, though matriarch of the series Annie Sugden (played by respected actress Sheila Mercier, sister of Brian Rix) was offered a two-year tenure. She has been there ever since.

It had only taken six months from the first screening of 'Emmerdale Farm' on Monday, 16 October 1972 for it to become the success story of the new ITV afternoon network. An evening hour-long omnibus was soon being shown in many regions, bringing the series to a new audience that would eventually claim it as a peak-time soap. Reviews were glowing, the *Yorkshire Post*'s critic describing it as 'one of the most authentic series I have ever seen'. The earliest recorded audience figures showed that some 2,203,000 viewers agreed.

With the departure of his screen brother, Joe Sugden (played by Frazer Hines) was the undisputed 'Emmerdale' sex symbol – and promptly married milk-recorder Christine Sharp (played by Angela Cheyne). The marriage did not last, but its trials and tribulations established Joe in the hearts of many, as well as boosting the viewing figures – as have many other soap weddings before and since.

Producers David Goddard, Peter Holman and Robert Cardona (who presided over 270 episodes) had come and gone before the appointment in November 1976 of Michael Glynn marked a change of pace. He had made his reputation in 'Z-Cars', and he introduced many more characters to ease the strain on the Sugdens. He also made wider use of the countryside, introduced a newspaper, the *Hotten Courier* (Yorkshire Television printed copies with real-life 'Emmerdale' news to distribute as press releases), and brought in more topical contemporary references such as Beckindale's 1977 street-party to celebrate the Queen's Silver Jubilee – a celebration that mirrored similar events in every community in Britain.

Big moves were also afoot in 1976 with a change of location: residents in Arncliffe, the village originally chosen for outside filming, had not bargained for the notoriety that descended, and a new village was selected to depict Beckindale. The major problem with this was the loss of the village's most recognisable location: the Woolpack. Craftily, this changed location, too, owing to supposed 'structural damage'.

Many future star names have passed through 'Emmerdale' as minor characters: in the mid-seventies Joanne Whalley played young Angela a decade before her big-screen portrayal of Christine Keeler; while Beverley Callard – better-known as 'Coronation Street' barmaid Liz McDonald – played one of Jackie Merrick's many girlfriends in the eighties.

The year 1977 saw the arrival of a very much more permanent character in Dolly Acaster. Along with Jack Sugden, Dolly was to be played by two people over the course of her stay, the first being Katherine Barker.

The unmistakable figure of Richard Thorp was to be seen for the first time in 1982 when Alan Turner arrived as manager for NY Estates. Richard came to 'Emmerdale' with a long and impressive pedigree in television (Dr Rennie in 'Emergency – Ward 10') and in films (*The Dam Busters*), and is still going strong a decade later. This was a longer stint than his first soap spell in the seventies as sailor Doug Randall in 'Crossroads', but much had to do with the allure of the countryside. 'I am having the most incredible love-affair with Yorkshire,' he confesses. 'I will never go back to live in the South.'

Turner's arrival, together with that of the Merricks – Pat (Helen Weir) and children Sandie (Jane Hutcheson) and

Jackie (Ian Sharrock) – and the introduction of caretaker-turned-gamekeeper Seth Armstrong (played by Stan Richards) as a permanent character, was at the suggestion of Anne Gibbons, producer from 1979 to 1983. She increased the stock of regular characters in order to increase the amount of dramatic continuing storylines that could be woven around them – increasing, if you like, the 'must watch' factor. As a result, several peripheral characters bowed out in a reversal of earlier tactics. Richard Handford, who suc-

The Merrick family – Jackie, Sandie and mother Pat – arrived in 1980.

ceeded Anne Gibbons, built on this by increasing the number of scenes per episode to make the plot faster-moving, as well as giving the central characters more room to shine. Handford would also stir up a hornets' nest with the affair between Jack Sugden and Karen Moore.

Jack was now very much back in the series, and his romance with Pat Merrick had been rekindled: the love-story the scriptwriters had so carefully arranged to end in marriage was mirrored by the actors in real life – despite the on-screen straying! Jackie Merrick, Pat's son, proved a popular addition to the cast: four thousand fans turned up to witness

actor Ian Sharrock's real-life wedding in Leeds in 1985.

In 1982, Matt and Dolly, now married, added Samuel David to the family. His christening was broadcast on 6 May 1983, the 800th episode of 'Emmerdale'. Child actor Benjamin Whitehead joined the cast to play the role. His casting – at just a week old – came from a chance meeting on a train between Jean Rogers and an 'Emmerdale' fan who 'volunteered' a friend's child for the role. He continued for nine years until Jean's part was written out and Sam 'departed to Norfolk' with his screen mum.

Many a headline was made with the departure of Joe Sugden to work for NY Estates in France, having been rejected by vicar's daughter Barbara Peters (played by Rosie Kerslake). In reality, a just-married Frazer Hines was keen to explore other options after a decade in the series. He would return in 1986 to take over the reins as regional manager of NY Estates, beating Turner for the job and becoming the boss of his old boss.

The death of Toke Townley in 1984 robbed not only 'Emmerdale' of Sam Pearson but also the cast of a much-

Emmerdale celebrates its 1,000th episode in style as 'This is Your Life' host Eamonn Andrews surprises Sheila Mercier.

loved friend and colleague. It also inevitably weakened some of the 'Emmerdale' connections with Harvest Festival and other long-standing traditions that a man of his generation would uphold.

From modest beginnings 'Emmerdale' was now very much in the public eye. Being a peak-time evening soap helped, of course: as its popularity grew, it had moved from lunchtimes to late afternoons to an evening berth, though Thames held out until 1985.

The 1,000th episode, broadcast around this time, was celebrated in a unique way when Eamonn Andrews appeared to present Sheila Mercier with the big red book of 'This Is Your Life'.

The mid-eighties saw an influx of much new blood in the form of the Bates family – Caroline, together with children Kathy and Nick. Caroline Bates (played by Diana Davies) was scheduled for just twenty episodes but so entranced the writers that she was retained indefinitely; while both her screen children (played by Malandra Burrows and Cy Chadwick) are of course still major characters today. Eric Pollard (played by Christopher Chittell) arrived as manager and auctioneer at Hotten Market.

Helen Weir, alias Mrs Clive Hornby.

Pat Sugden's death in a car crash in 1986 catapulted the soap into the kind of hard-hitting drama that had been lacking, critics claimed, for a long time. When Helen Weir (in real life Mrs Clive Hornby) fell pregnant, naturally her screen character did likewise. Helen then bowed out, leaving Clive to act some very harrowing scenes. Screen son Robert remained.

Pat Sugden's funeral was one of the first challenges to meet new producer Michael Russell, familiar with 'Emmerdale' through having written for it. He would go on to bring in such topical stories as nuclear dumping on Pencross Fell (protesting against which landed Jack in prison) and Dolly's long-forgotten illegitimate son who, now aged eighteen, deserted from the Army and arrived in Beckindale seeking his mother. 'We never preach,' insisted Russell of his controversial twists to the story. 'We tell the story and let the viewers make their own judgements.'

On 5 January 1988, 'Emmerdale Farm' had achieved a programming milestone – being transmitted country-wide on the same day at the same time. After fifteen years, this was a major achievement. The year was also the first in which broadcasting continued through Christmas.

In 1988 producer Stuart Doughty, a graduate from 'Brookside', arrived as the eighth producer of the series. 'Evolution not revolution' was his watchword, though he conceded that 'we can't ignore the other soaps; we have to be competitive'. To this end, 'Emmerdale Farm' began – imperceptibly at first – to lose some of its farming content; and in 1989 it finally dropped the word 'Farm' from its title.

As the pace picked up once more, 1989 saw the departure of several well-known figures. The loss of Frederick Pyne, who had played Matt Skilbeck since the first episode, to the theatre in November was quite a shock; while Hugh Manning, better-known as the Reverend Donald Hinton, the longest-serving of the clerics, also took his leave. St Mary's Church has not had a resident vicar since. As if that was not enough, Jackie Merrick was written out in August after a shotgun accident. This was a daring decision since Jackie was one of the most popular characters and a prominent representative of the younger generation of 'Emmerdale'.

Joe and Kate Sugden (Frazer Hines and Sally Knyvette) with Kate's teenage children Rachel and Mark Hughes (Glenda and Craig McKay). Their domestic bliss was to be short-lived.

Jackie's sister Sandie Merrick and her daughter Louise moved to Scotland, leaving the door open for her to return at some future date. Jackie Merrick's death left wife Kathy a widow, and 1989 saw the first sighting of her future husband, Christopher Tate (played by Peter Amory), as one of the newly arrived, *nouveaux riches* Tates. Actor Norman Bowler was a well-known face even before assuming the role of Frank Tate, the new owner of Home Farm. He had enjoyed a successful television career as detective Harry Hawkins in 'Softly Softly'. Claire King, who plays his wife

Kim Tate, gave up life as a punk rocker to move up-market.

Manchester-based Diana Davies took a break from trans-Pennine travel when her character, Mrs Bates, moved to Scarborough in 1990, a romantic liaison with Alan Turner having fallen through. She would, however, return in 1992. Her departure opened the door for the Feldmann family: mother Elizabeth (Kate Dove) and children Elsa and Michael. Elsa (Naomi Lewis) departed, but Michael (Matthew Vaughan) is still very much around as part of the new 'young image' of 'Emmerdale'. In 1992, indeed, a scantily clad Michael and screen girlfriend Rachel Hughes were to be seen advertising 'Emmerdale' to a new generation of viewers in teen magazines under the heading 'You learn about sex earlier in the country'.

Elizabeth Feldmann was to become a leading character; and for actress Kate Dove it was quite a turn-around, having survived a motorway accident in the mid eighties by determination, the surgeons' skill and sheer good fortune. She showed similar tenacity in auditioning for the part just four months later.

With the departure of several key characters, the stage was set for actor Tony Pitts as Archie Brooks to return after a spell in Hotten and establish a major role after floating in and out for several years. Sarah Connolly (played by Madeleine Howard), who had arrived as the mobile librarian, also took a bigger role, moving into the farm annexe as Jack's girlfriend and nailing up the connecting door!

The arrival of the Hughes family – Kate, with children Rachel and Mark – in 1988 proved a far-reaching decision. Kate (played by Sally Knyvette) captured Joe Sugden's heart, then departed in the most unfortunate circumstances after a

Philandering Pete Whiteley, played by Jim Millea.

road accident involving Pete Whiteley (played by Jim Millea) – the married man with whom teenaged daughter Rachel (played by Glenda McKay) was having an affair. After her release from gaol, Sally Knyvette left the series. Glenda and real-life brother Craig are still fixtures of the 'Emmerdale' scene – as is Pete Whiteley's widow, Lynn (played by Fionnuala Ellwood), and her son Peter – one of the three child characters, currently seen alongside Alice Bates and Robert Sugden.

Dolly Skilbeck's departure in 1991 after ten years provoked thousands of viewers' letters. Sadder still was the death of Arthur Pentelow, who, as Henry Wilks, had established himself as a fixture from the beginning of the series, latterly as Amos Brearly's partner at the Woolpack. Ronald Magill, who had played Amos from the very beginning, had already decided to retire from the series, leaving the way clear for Alan Turner to move in behind the bar. Since Sarah's move to Emmerdale Farm, Alan has been assisted by comely barmaid Carol (played by Philomena McDonagh).

Barring real-life tragedy, the arrival and departure of actors from 'Emmerdale' can be voluntary or enforced, decisions taken year by year at the whim of the producer. The woman in charge of shaping 'Emmerdale' in the nineties is Morag Bain, who includes script editor for 'EastEnders' in an impressive track record. She has outlined her view of the programme in her foreword; but, as to future comings and goings, you will just have to stay tuned to find out!

The grey stones of Emmerdale Farm have stood the ravages of time for over one hundred years. The current incumbent, Jack Sugden, would be very happy if he thought the next hundred years would see as little change. But, if Emmerdale Farm should ever fall into the hands of his brother Joe, change would inevitably follow.

BECKINDALE

BECKINDALE is the village where the majority of the 'Emmerdale' characters have their home. The Woolpack (see page 72) and the Malt Shovel are the village's two hostelries. Close to the Woolpack is the post office, where Seth collects his pension. Seth lives at 6 Demdyke Row, some 400 yards from the centre of Beckindale, with his wife Meg – just along from number 3, where Kathy and Jackie Merrick once lived. Dolly bought number 3 in 1990, and Nick and Alice Bates currently reside there with live-in babyminder Archie Brooks.

The main street passes the village hall – venue for many a theatrical production in the past – and the village bowling green. A path leads through the graveyard to St Mary's Church, where the Reverend Donald Hinton presided until his retirement in 1989. Since then, services have been held in rotation with three other local churches. Church Lane, on to which St Mary's faces, also has a playing-field and a children's playground.

Number 17 Main Street is the Beckindale Fish and Game Farm office, as well as home for Elizabeth Feldmann who has been running the administra-

The post office cum corner shop, hub of Beckindale's commercial life.

The cottages at Demdyke Row have housed many a controversial character.

Home Farm has traditionally been Beckindale's biggest single source of employment – something Frank Tate's holiday village has continued.

tive side of the operation for Alan Turner since Caroline Bates left for Scarborough. It is directly opposite the Woolpack, which makes it convenient for employee Seth Armstrong to combine business with pleasure.

The village grew up around the local farms – principally the Home Farm estate, which was the area's biggest employer. The nearest town is Hotten, six miles away, where Mark and Melanie studied at the comprehensive. Bus services outside school hours are sporadic, however, and with the last bus returning at 9.30 p.m. parents are always busy ferrying their offspring hither and yon.

The Making of 'Emmerdale'

For twenty years, the attraction of 'Emmerdale' has always been the great outdoors, so it is no surprise to learn that half the series is shot outside the studio.

Opposite: *the mill studios at Farsley*
Below: *Kathy, Joe and Annie wait their cue as sound and light levels are checked.*

Aside from special events which may take place in Hotten, the fictitious near-by town (represented by Otley), or in Leeds (where Rachel is at university), action takes place in one of three locations: either in the studio, on the farm or in Beckindale.

Since 1989, the studio has been in a

The Green Room at Farsley, where actors relax between takes and learn their lines.

converted mill at Farsley in Leeds, where the individual sets representing such familiar scenes as the farm kitchen and the Woolpack bar are all laid out. The studio scenes for four episodes at a time are all shot in a block (lasting a fortnight) for which period the cast regard the mill as their 'home'; this follows a similar spell on location at the farm or the village.

The indoor scenes shot in the studio will not usually bear much resemblance to the finished programme since the outdoor action will be edited in between them. Indeed, they may bear little relation to the order in which they are screened – and this can be even more confusing when a 'double strand' is being worked in which two completely different story-lines are being pursued by two different directors. Not surprisingly, there are rehearsal facilities where everything can be honed to perfection on Monday

Designing the scenes for such prime locations as the Woolpack and the farm kitchen.

Chris Chittell (Eric Pollard) prepares for broadcast action outside the Woolpack.

and Tuesday before the scenes that are to take place in each particular indoor location are shot in the remaining three days of the week.

Shooting involves an army of people from the director and the producer to cameramen to lighting controllers, sound technicians, make-up and wardrobe assistants – even a carpenter is at hand in case adjustments need to be made to the scenery. One of the most important jobs involves continuity: if Alan Turner is wearing, say, a flower in his buttonhole on entering the Woolpack (an outdoor shot in the village that represents Beckindale), then he must be wearing a similar bloom when he enters the studio set through the pub door. Anything less than perfection on this score would ruin the illusion.

Yorkshire Television has pledged never to name the village it uses to portray Beckindale. The farm which represents Emmerdale Farm is actually seven miles away but otherwise very few changes are made from the reality. Until 1991, the Commercial Inn had to acquire a new name and sign over the door when filming began but now it has been officially renamed the Woolpack.

While the identity of the village is an official secret, fans inevitably locate Beckindale's real-life location, and a local tea-room does a roaring trade in 'Emmerdale' souvenirs along with its traditional Yorkshire fare. For the duration of filming, the village hall houses dressing and make-up facilities for the actors and production crew.

On the farm, care had to be taken that the everyday work of 'Farmer Bell', as he was known, was not hindered. An inch-thick sheaf of programme notes, constantly updated, keeps the production crew abreast of farming practices and methods, and these have already been taken into account when the series is written: hence lambing and harvesting will always be seen at the appropriate time of the year. Every month means a different job down on the farm; and, as you would expect, 'Emmerdale' reflects

Above: *setting up the lights for an outside broadcast.*
Opposite: *the wardrobe room at Farsley, stocked with town and country clothing.*

this to the letter, from hay-making to muck-spreading.

When filming away from the studio, a fleet of vehicles is needed to transport the production team to location. There's also an electrical generator, a wardrobe van and – most important when out on the windswept Dales – a canteen. Outside broadcasts have become considerably less difficult during the twenty-year history of 'Emmerdale' with the

Clive Hornby and Madeleine Howard consult with production staff on location.

march of technology: the advent of lighter cameras, now using video tape rather than film, is just one example. Today's cameras are not much heavier than the camcorders viewers use for their home videos.

Occasional venues where OB (outside broadcasts) may be made include the fish farm, Hotten Market (represented by Otley Market) and the Woolpack cellar (an old wool-store on the ground floor of the Farsley mill studios), while Tate Haulage is in Leeds where scenes in the yard and in Christopher Tate's office are filmed at Farsley, near to the mill.

In the past scenes have been filmed at such real-life events as York and Wetherby racecourses (Joe being a man of the turf – as is Frazer Hines, the man who plays him), the Great Yorkshire Show and Bridlington beach. All this adds to the feeling of reality – as does the occasional cameo appearance, such as one made by the legendary Yorkshire and England fast bowler Fred Trueman.

Other events have utilised the Yorkshire countryside, such as fell racing at Kilnsey Crag – where Frazer Hines

The Gallery at the mill studio, where vision mixing and production matters are decided.

competed with real athletes – and the pot-hole rescue where Matt Skilbeck (actor Frederick Pyne) went underground to rescue a trapped Scandinavian.

The most dramatic scenes ever broadcast in 'Emmerdale' were undoubtedly those in 1988 when Crossgill, the farmhouse that was to be Matt and Dolly's new home, was set ablaze owing to the carelessness of Phil Pearce – and with Annie Sugden trapped inside. A derelict house high in the Pennines was used, with fifty-six smoke-generators situated inside the house, tin foil and red spotlights simultaneously simulating flames behind windows, while car tyres and straw were set alight outside the house to provide a deathly pall of black smoke overhead. Amazingly, the scene was accomplished in a single take – evidence once more of the professionalism of the 'Emmerdale' production team.

It is this that makes the finished product, assembled from a jigsaw of outdoor and indoor footage, the compulsive watching it has remained for two decades.

CONNELTON

CONNELTON, situated to the west of Beckindale, is a larger village of perhaps 1,500 inhabitants. Its original residents were local tin-miners, and the success of this activity led to prosperity and the building of several public houses, two churches and a library. With a supermarket and a range of shops, it is often used by people from Beckindale and the surrounding area as a handy shopping centre, while the Feathers is a popular restaurant with the younger set (Joe and Kate met there). Connelton is also where Beckindale's younger inhabitants, including Robert Sugden, go to infant and junior school.

HOTTEN

HOTTEN is Beckindale's nearest market-town, with a population of over 12,000. Its newspaper, the long-established *Hotten Courier*, covers local news and views. As well as the cattle-market and wool-distribution centre that mark Hotten's position of importance in the commercial world, the town also boasts a theatre and an art gallery for the culturally inclined.

The area's long connection with sheep-farming is celebrated by the Weaving Museum in Distaff Row. The area's secondary school is also situated in Hotten, with a regular bus service from Beckindale and surrounding areas.

The Story So Far

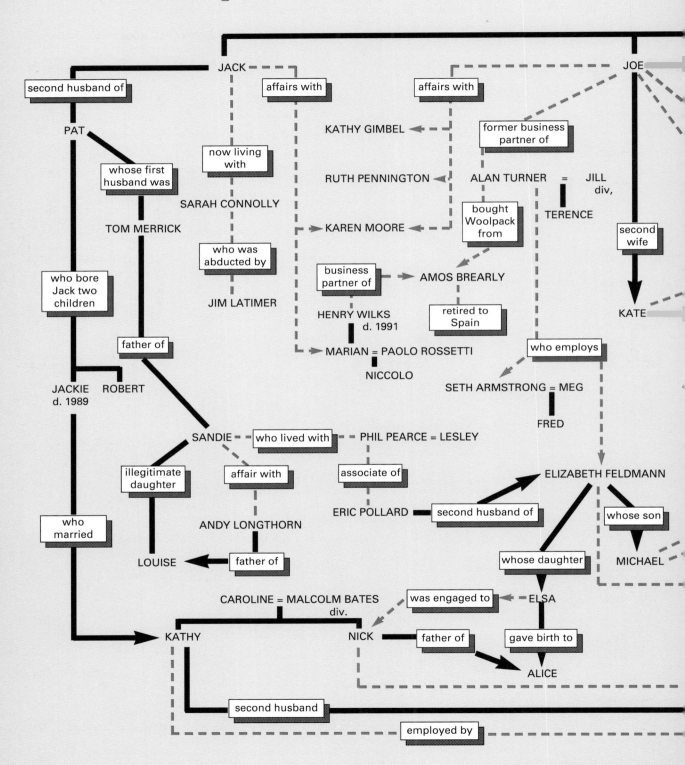

SAM PEARSON = MARY (née ARMITAGE)
d. 1984   d. 1968

JACK --- affairs with   affairs with   JOE

second husband of   KATHY GIMBEL ◄---   former business partner of

PAT   whose first husband was   RUTH PENNINGTON ◄   ALAN TURNER = JILL div,

             now living with   bought Woolpack from   TERENCE

SARAH CONNOLLY   KAREN MOORE ◄---   second wife

TOM MERRICK   who was abducted by   business partner of ► AMOS BREARLY   KATE

who bore Jack two children   JIM LATIMER   HENRY WILKS d. 1991   retired to Spain

             father of   MARIAN = PAOLO ROSSETTI   who employs

JACKIE d. 1989   ROBERT   NICCOLO   SETH ARMSTRONG = MEG

SANDIE --- who lived with --- PHIL PEARCE = LESLEY   FRED

illegitimate daughter   affair with   associate of   ELIZABETH FELDMANN

who married   ERIC POLLARD ▬ second husband of ►   whose son

ANDY LONGTHORN   MICHAEL

LOUISE ◄ father of   whose daughter

CAROLINE = MALCOLM BATES div.   was engaged to ◄ ELSA

KATHY   NICK ▬ father of   gave birth to

        second husband   ALICE

        employed by

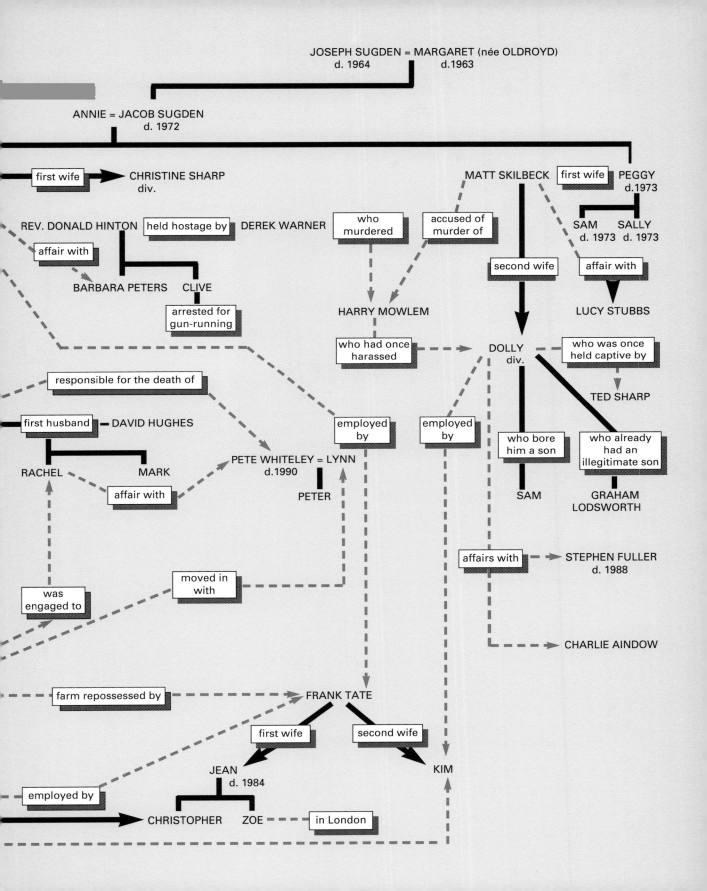

JOSEPH SUGDEN = MARGARET (née OLDROYD)
d. 1964   d.1963

ANNIE = JACOB SUGDEN
d. 1972

first wife → CHRISTINE SHARP
div.

MATT SKILBECK   first wife   PEGGY
d.1973

SAM   SALLY
d. 1973   d. 1973

REV. DONALD HINTON   held hostage by   DEREK WARNER   who murdered   accused of murder of

affair with

BARBARA PETERS   CLIVE   second wife   affair with

arrested for gun-running   LUCY STUBBS

HARRY MOWLEM

who had once harassed   DOLLY   who was once held captive by
div.

responsible for the death of   TED SHARP

first husband   DAVID HUGHES   employed by   employed by   who bore him a son   who already had an illegitimate son

RACHEL   MARK   PETE WHITELEY = LYNN   SAM   GRAHAM LODSWORTH
d.1990

affair with   PETER

was engaged to   moved in with   affairs with   STEPHEN FULLER
d. 1988

CHARLIE AINDOW

farm repossessed by   FRANK TATE

first wife   second wife

employed by   JEAN   KIM
d. 1984

CHRISTOPHER   ZOE   in London

C H A R L I E   A I N D O W

CHARLIE AINDOW is a councillor who believes in getting the most gain out of his position. His covert business partnership with Eric Pollard typified the two men's devious nature as they diverted promising antiques offered at Hotten Market to their own clients and pocketed a substantial profit.

David Fleeshman was born in Leeds forty years ago. He was educated and trained in the profession in Birmingham and made his professional début with the Birmingham Rep in 1973. His television appearances have included 'Boys from the Black-stuff', 'Bulman' and the Ruth Rendell mysteries. On the large screen he appeared in Pink Floyd's *The Wall*.

Aindow also showed himself up in a bad light when he had an affair with Dolly Skilbeck, made her pregnant, and deserted her in her hour of need. He continues to be a thorn in the side of Frank Tate and his former colleague in corruption Eric Pollard.

David, who is keen on swimming and photography, is married to Sue Jenkins, probably best-known as barmaid Gloria Todd in 'Coronation Street'. They have two children.

S E T H   A R M S T R O N G

SETH ARMSTRONG is the classic poacher-turned-gamekeeper and is up to every trick in the book.

With Alan Turner as his boss, Seth has to keep on his toes, but he is usually one step ahead of his employer by dint of his native cunning. In company with Archie Brooks, Nick Bates, Carol Nelson and anyone else who is game, Seth plots and schemes – and it is usually against Alan Turner that he conspires.

Seth lives in Demdyke Row with his wife, Meg, and his dog, Smokey. Recently eligible for his pension, Seth was so worried that Turner might see him as 'past it' that he concealed his new-found wealth at the game farm, faked amnesia and all but got himself sacked for dishonesty in 'stealing' back his own money – discovered and retained by Turner, who awaited Seth's 'confession'. He confessed, and was assured by Turner that he was too valuable a gamekeeper to be discarded just because he had reached sixty-five.

Stan Richards, who was born in Barnsley sixty-two years ago, worked in clubs and cabaret before being 'discovered' by Ken Loach in 1975 and taking up acting. He then appeared in 'Coronation Street', 'Crown Court', 'The Cuckoo Waltz', 'Last of the Summer Wine' and 'All Creatures Great and Small'. He joined the cast of 'Emmerdale' in March 1978.

Stan has been married to Sue for forty years and has three sons, three grandsons and one great-grandson. He describes himself as 'tall, dark and two out of three can't be bad!'

CAROLINE BATES

CAROLINE BATES now lives in Scarborough with her ailing mother, but returns to Beckindale quite frequently to help out son Nick with his difficult domestic situation and keep a motherly eye on daughter Kathy, now married into the volatile Tate family.

She also assists Alan Turner, to whom she was once engaged to be married, and who frequently uses her services – waitressing in the restaurant and helping him through the many traumas that are part of his life. Alan still has a soft spot for her, but often takes outrageous liberties with her easygoing nature.

Diana Davies claims no formal theatrical training, but a list of her television appearances is a roll-call of signal success, including 'Coronation Street', 'Juliet Bravo', 'Shoestring' and 'A Family at War'. On stage she has appeared with Glenda Jackson in *Rose* and in a number of pantomimes.

NICK BATES

NICK BATES did not find life easy when his girlfriend Elsa Feldmann, tired of life in Beckindale, left him and their baby, Alice, for a life in the big city. Young Nick was left with problems on all fronts.

Elsa's hire-purchase debts, Alice's upbringing and maintaining his job as gardener at Home Farm all contributed to making Nick's life extremely difficult. Even with the help of his mother, Caroline Bates, and Elsa's mother, Elizabeth Feldmann, things were proving extremely hard for a young man of twenty-three who should have been having the time of his life.

Now, with Archie Brooks taking over on the home front, Nick is more able

to enjoy his life; and, apart from the recent drama when a distraught woman claimed that baby Alice really belonged to her, things are fine for Nick Bates.

Cy Chadwick played the drums at theatre school but opted for an acting career when Yorkshire Television cast him in 'The Book Tower' and, later, the children's programme 'How We Used to Live'. He left school at sixteen, and a part in the film *On the Boat* led to an 'Emmerdale' audition and the role of Nick Bates, which he took up in September 1985. Seven years later, he picked up the threads of his musical career with a single, 'The Love Game'.

AMOS BREARLY

AMOS BREARLY, the bewhiskered landlord at the Woolpack, was one of Beckindale's landmarks from the end of the war until his retirement in 1991. A bachelor, he shared his pub – sometimes reluctantly – with Henry Wilks, but enjoyed the affections of many. He now lives in retirement in Spain.

Ronald Magill was for nine years a director and actor at the Nottingham Playhouse, and he has adapted plays by Goldoni and Molière. His television appearances include 'Special Branch' and 'Parkin's Patch'.

ARCHIE BROOKS

ARCHIE BROOKS was at one time an out-and-out tearaway of no fixed abode and generally regarded as a scrounger going nowhere.

When he set off to see the world, few thought he would be back. However, he returned a new man – more responsible, teetotal, and with a new ecological awareness previously unremarked in his character. He also confessed that his travels had taken him no further than Leicester Forest East service station.

In spite of his workshy attitude, Archie has a good heart and generally likes to help those in need – like once emotionally distressed Lynn Whiteley and harassed Nick Bates.

Romantically Archie still carries a torch for Zoë Tate, Frank's daughter, even though she has now left the area and was last seen involved with an older man.

Nowadays Archie shares a home with Nick Bates where he has finally earned the respect of all in his position as child minder to baby Alice.

Tony Pitts has one main interest in life apart from giving substance and credibility to the multi-faceted character of

Archie Brooks, and that is football – both playing and supporting. He is a keen fan of Sheffield Wednesday and must have taken great pleasure in their success during the 1991–2 season.

Tony's other interests include motor sport and wining and dining. Born in Sheffield in 1962, he was a truck mechanic before taking up acting.

THE REVEREND TONY CHARLTON

THE REVEREND TONY CHARLTON was a curate, succeeding Donald Hinton. His first task, in 1990, was to bury Pete Whiteley. Often seen without his dog collar, his unconventional manner made him popular with the younger generation. He left in 1991 after a brief 'liaison' with Kathy Merrick.

Stephen Rashbrook recently spent a day in women's clothes while filming 'Move Over, Darling' for the BBC. However, when he returned home to his wife Alaine and children Oliver and Sophie they found nothing had changed.

Recently Stephen has appeared as Laertes in *Hamlet* at the National Theatre and as Oliver in *As You Like It* at the Greenwich Theatre, and he has also appeared in the Royal Shakespeare Company's *Nicholas Nickleby*.

SARAH CONNOLLY

SARAH CONNOLLY lives with Jack Sugden at Emmerdale Farm. Before moving in with Jack, who by agreement proposes to her every year, she ran a mobile library for the council.

On arriving at Emmerdale she immediately sealed off the connecting door between the farm cottage she shared with Jack and the main farm accommodation where Annie ruled.

Time has seen a great change, and Sarah is now a key member of the Emmerdale team as she not only serves as mother to Jack's son Robert and looks after the home, but also puts in a full day's work on the farm, including early-morning milking.

Madeleine Howard was born in Harrow and lives in London, but while working shares a rented house in Leeds with Fionnuala Ellwood. Before joining 'Emmerdale' – initially for only seven episodes as a librarian romantically linked with Jack Sugden – Madeleine appeared in Thames Television's drama 'Gems'.

In her spare time Madeleine is studying Alexander Technique teaching, which she believes helps her enormously in life and in her acting.

ELIZABETH FELDMANN

ELIZABETH FELDMANN and her two children, Michael and Elsa, lost their farm which they had struggled to maintain since her husband's death when Frank Tate forced them to sell up. When he bought Home Farm, and with it the ownership of the Feldmann farm, it quickly became apparent to Tate that the farm was a totally unviable proposition, and the Feldmanns' home went under the hammer.

Fortunately Alan Turner came to the rescue – not entirely without self-interest – and gave them a roof over their heads as part of his plan to have the efficient Elizabeth at his beck and call in his little empire of the Woolpack and the trout and game enterprises.

Sensibly Elizabeth does not allow herself to be dominated, especially now she has a new, more important man in her life.

Kate Dove is a trained operatic soprano who has also taken part in an escapology act. While she seems unlikely to need the former talent in 'Emmerdale', the latter may be of great benefit now that she is married to Eric Pollard.

Away from 'Emmerdale', Kate, who trained at the Triangle Theatre Workshop, New York, and lived for four years in Manhattan, has done theatre work (both acting and directing) and had other television parts.

MICHAEL FELDMANN

MICHAEL FELDMANN is the good guy gone wrong. Recently a trusted member of the Emmerdale workforce with a steady relationship and marriage plans involving Rachel Hughes, he now awaits trial for aggravated burglary and is bailed to live with his new lover, Lynn Whiteley, at Whiteley's Farm. Michael has always been headstrong and rebellious, but he reached the bottom of the pit after Rachel called off their engagement. Things can only improve.

Matthew Vaughan did theatre work and some small film parts before returning to Sheffield and involving himself in an actors' co-operative. It was while working there that the Yorkshire-born actor was offered the part of Michael Feldmann as one of the new intake in 'Emmerdale', joining the series in late 1989.

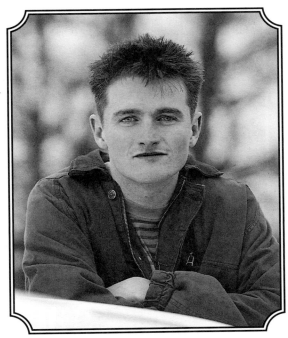

THE REVEREND DONALD HINTON

DONALD HINTON was the last full-time clergyman to preside at St Mary's Church, and officiated at the wedding of Joe and Kate during his decade in Beckindale. He retired to Coventry in 1989.

Hugh Manning has acted in more than twenty Shake-speare plays and has played the lead in many other West End productions. He worked with Noël Coward in *The Apple Cart* in London in 1953. His television appearances include 'Mrs Thursday', 'The Sullivan Brothers', 'The Avengers' and 'Poldark'. He has been President of Equity and was a founder member of an arts advisory group for the Labour Party.

MARK HUGHES

MARK HUGHES is another victim of Kate Sugden's tragedy, but somehow has the ability to take that setback, and all others that come his way, with a pinch of salt.

Mark is younger than Rachel in years and a lot younger in attitude. When they took over the cottage at Emmerdale, after Jack and Sarah moved into the farmhouse, he could not wait to repaint it in garish colours and organise parties with loud music and boisterous behaviour.

Rachel was quick to spot what was going on and posted her fiancé, Michael Feldmann, to take up residence and keep an eye on him while she was away.

When his studies proved a failure owing to a lack of effort, he took a job at the holiday village. After a brief romance with Melanie Clifford ended he took up with Lisa, a woman of thirtyish, who probably furthered his education a lot more than his original plan to go to Glasgow University would have done.

Craig McKay believes his lack of theatrical training will be obviously apparent to viewers of 'Emmerdale', but actually he handles the part of Mark Hughes and all his troubles very convincingly.

Craig is $1\frac{1}{2}$ years younger than sister Glenda, but they were both thrown in at the deep end together and Craig acquitted himself equally well. His only previous experience was two small child parts for Yorkshire Television and a paper round.

In his leisure hours Craig plays badminton, squash and snooker.

RACHEL HUGHES

RACHEL HUGHES came to Beckindale from Sheffield when her mother, Kate, married Joe Sugden and moved into Emmerdale Farm. She and her brother, Mark, took a while to settle in and accept Joe (not least because he had shot their dog for sheep-worrying) but soon became part of Beckindale's younger set.

Apart from the notoriety the affair with Pete Whiteley brought her, she then had to face the loss of her mother – first to prison on a manslaughter charge for the death of Pete Whiteley and then again when Kate returned to Emmerdale so scarred by the shame of what she had done and by the prison experience that she could not remain with her family.

Now she has broken off her engagement to Michael Feldmann and she is un-attached but enjoying her emancipated life in her second year at Leeds University.

Glenda McKay was born in Jimmy's hospital, Leeds, on 2 February 1971. She had no formal theatre training apart from A-level theatre studies at school, and at one time was a checkout girl at a supermarket.

'Emmerdale' was her first big break, and the schoolgirl temptress of Pete Whiteley really proved to be a part to get her teeth into.

Glenda and her brother Craig (who plays her screen brother Mark) come from a Scottish family on their father's side, and their mother is from Hull. Glenda believes in keeping trim by regular workouts in the gym and a lot of hill walking.

THE HONOURABLE NEIL KINCAID

THE HONOURABLE NEIL KINCAID cuts quite a dash about Beckindale with his stately home and successful City stockbroking business. During the week he is a wheeler-dealer in London, but to relax he returns to Yorkshire at weekends where he takes up his interest in horses and riding.

When Kim Tate broke her leg he proved to be of great assistance, even supplying his own labour to help out. Unfortunately recent events have proved him to be not totally honourable, and Frank Tate may well rue the day he came into his life.

Brian Deacon as City slicker Neil Kincaid is always seen around horses, but in real life Brian is just a little nervous in their presence after a recent fall. He feels that 'Emmerdale', which calls for frequent riding and horse-handling scenes, is therapeutic. Apart from horsemanship, Brian, who is unmarried, is a very keen golfer.

SERGEANT IAN MACARTHUR

SERGEANT IAN MacARTHUR was the Hotten-based policeman who, from 1980, covered the local village beat. He was present at many incidents, such as Nick Bates's confession to having appropriated part of the haul from the post office robbery, Kate Sugden's fatal driving accident and the Home Farm fire. When Jackie Merrick accidentally killed himself, MacArthur took Kathy and Joe to identify the body. A kindly, sympathetic, caring policeman of the old school.

Martin Dale has recently been obliged to take time off after undergoing heart surgery. Yorkshire Television kindly wrote MacArthur out while Martin recovered; but he reappeared in good health to investigate the burglary at Home Farm. Away from 'Emmerdale', Martin, who lives in Wakefield with his wife Diane, does regular theatre work and sings in cabaret.

JACKIE MERRICK

JACKIE MERRICK was the illegitimate son of Jack Sugden and Pat Harker. After a rebellious youth, he survived a car crash to learn farming skills and to mature. He died in 1989 after a shooting accident, leaving wife Kathy (née Bates) a widow in her early twenties

Ian Sharrock, who as Jackie Merrick met a violent death at the wrong end of a shotgun, has been very busy since leaving 'Emmerdale'. His most recent engagement was in an NBC production filmed at Pinewood called 'Sarah', based on the lives of the Duke and Duchess of York. Ian is married to Pam and has two children, William and Natalie.

SANDIE MERRICK

SANDIE MERRICK was the teenaged daughter of Pat who fell pregnant and gave birth to a daughter (adopted) before coming under the Emmerdale roof when her mother married Jack Sugden. After working at Hotten Market (where she became manager) and a spell living with ne'er-do-well Phil Pearce, she left for Scotland to live with her father and adopt her now-parentless child Louise.

Jane Hutcheson was born in Stockport and studied drama at Birmingham University and then worked in repertory.

Her television work has included 'Coronation Street', 'A Family at War' and 'How We Used to Live'.

BILL MIDDLETON

BILL MIDDLETON used to be inseparable from his partner in crime Jock MacDonald, who is not to be seen around nowadays after he set fire to the barn at Home Farm and let Michael Feldmann take the blame. Bill was never a willing aide to Jock's villainy and is now happy to join Seth in a pint and make Alan Turner's life a misery as the pair of them seize on every possible opportunity to belittle or make fun of him.

Apart from his widowed mother, Bill has no family connections.

Johnny Caesar winces when he has to wear the Newcastle United scarf as Bill Middleton as he is actually a Sunderland supporter. Johnny trained as an engineer before becoming a guitarist with various pop groups in the sixties. Before joining 'Emmerdale', Johnny built up his acting experience with roles in 'Crown Court', 'The Practice' and 'Coronation Street'. He has also appeared as a stand-up comedian in cabaret and clubs.

CAROL NELSON

CAROL NELSON, with her big blue eyes, looks the picture of innocence as she dispenses drinks from behind the Woolpack bar. She's polite and chatty to everyone and always ready to listen to their problems, but files away all she sees and hears to prompt mischief and scandal in all directions.

She came to the Woolpack when Alan Turner advertised for a permanent barmaid after a succession of part-timers, including Caroline Bates and Elizabeth Feldmann proved less than adequate.

The arrival in Beckindale of her daughter Lorraine, whose wayward behaviour will do Carol's reputation no good at all, is bound to cramp her style; but the wise would do well to keep their secrets from Carol.

Philomena McDonagh came to 'Emmerdale' in 1991 after appearing in the theatre in a host of productions, including *Guys and Dolls*, *Hobson's Choice* and *Loot*. She has also appeared as Lady Macbeth and as Maria in *Twelfth Night*. On television she has appeared in 'Angels', 'Grange Hill', 'Families' and 'The Bill' – and most recently as the mother in the Instant PG Tea commercials.

LORRAINE NELSON

LORRAINE NELSON, barmaid Carol's daughter, is a real handful. Not only is she virtually beyond parental control, but she is also man-mad and has regularly pursued Mark Hughes, Michael Feldmann and Archie Brooks – to their great discomfort.

She is a great embarrassment to her mother who, as Beckindale's leading busybody, would revel in reporting her activities – if she were someone else's daughter.

Nicola Strong was a waitress and sold shoes at Dolcis before joining the cast as rebellious Lorraine Nelson, but after gaining an A level in theatre studies and a BTEC National Diploma in Performing Arts she had various colourful engagements during 1989–91. These have included parts such as Pretty Polly in *Mr Punch and the Pirates* and Nancy in *Gaslight*.

In her spare time Nicola has many interests including aerobics, swimming and abseiling. She also likes working with disabled people.

Still at home, she lives with her parents, Kathleen and Albert, and brother and sister, Neil and Michelle.

SAM PEARSON

SAM PEARSON, Annie Sugden's father, was a fixture at Emmerdale from the beginning, upholding old traditions and instructing new generations in country lore.

Toke Townley, who died suddenly in 1984, and who is still much missed in his role as the gentle old man steeped in rural traditions, did not actually like the countryside. He loved music and played the flute and the recorder – a skill he sometimes displayed as Sam Pearson in 'Emmerdale'.

ERIC POLLARD

ERIC POLLARD is the rascal who took over Sandie Merrick's job as auctioneer at Hotten Market. From this position, dodgy Eric was able to carry on his wheeling and dealing with a lot of inside knowledge.

Eric was the man to go to for almost anything saleable. Land, artefacts or live-stock – he would always come up with a bargain, and someone would always be the worse off. He has a ruthless streak, which was highlighted when he allowed Phil Pearce to go to prison when they were involved together in a scam to steal valuable fireplaces from Home Farm.

After a disastrous romance with Debbie Wilson, who turned the tables on him by flattering his ego, becoming engaged to him, and then running off with a consid-erable sum of money, he courted and won Elizabeth Feldmann despite her reserva-tions about his moral character and Michael Feldmann's long-maintained belief that Eric was out to con her. Eventually he promised Elizabeth to be a reformed character, promised Michael that he would love and honour his moth-er and advanced sufficiently in the esteem of the Feldmanns to marry into the family.

But with Eric Pollard...

Christopher Chittell is most unlike Eric Pollard in real life. It would be hard to imagine the dodgy auctioneer playing rugby or cricket or skin diving, but Christopher lists these amongst his favourite pastimes. On the large screen, Christopher, who with his definite mili-tary bearing hails from Aldershot, has appeared in *Zulu Dawn*, *The Charge of the Light Brigade* and a host of other films.

He lives with his wife Caroline and his two children, Benjamin and Rebecca.

DOLLY SKILBECK

DOLLY SKILBECK arrived in Beckindale in 1977 as Dolly Acaster. After a spell behind the Woolpack bar, she married Matt and they had a child, Sam. After an increasingly unhappy private life involving an affair with Stephen Fuller, she left Matt in 1988, and after a further affair with Charlie Aindow eventually moved to Norfolk with her son.

Jean Rogers (who took over the part from Katherine Barker) trained at the Guildhall School of Drama, and has worked with the National Theatre and the Chichester Festival Theatre. She has done a lot of radio work, including seven years with 'Listen with Mother'; and her television work has included 'George and Mildred', 'Crossroads', 'General Hospital' and 'Emergency – Ward 10'.

MATT SKILBECK

MATT SKILBECK became an honorary Sugden on his marriage to Peggy, but suffered a double blow when first his wife and then their twins died within a year. A second marriage to Dolly brought some happiness, but as their relationship disintegrated he became disillusioned and left for Norfolk at the end of 1989 – an uncharacteristic act from a dependable man.

Frederick Pyne studied at the Royal Academy of Dramatic Art and, as well as a lot of repertory work, he has appeared at the National Theatre and the Royal Court, working with some of Britain's most distinguished actors. His television

work includes parts in 'Dixon of Dock Green', 'Crossroads' and 'Justice'.

ANNIE SUGDEN

ANNIE SUGDEN still rules the roost as the elder stateswoman of Emmerdale Farm and head of the Sugden family. Both Jack and Joe know full well the power that lurks in her slender frame.

In times of crisis such as Kate's ordeal and the death of Henry Wilks, Annie makes the decisions in her own calm way, and she is usually right. As she recently told Mark Hughes when he got into trouble with his telephone bill, he had been daft – but he had still got a long way to go to match Jack and Joe. Annie has two good sons, but they certainly conspire to make things difficult for her and for themselves.

Amos's offer for her to spend her winters in Spain with him will probably give her a much-needed break from the rigours of life at Emmerdale Farm. The added fillip of a reunion with Leonard Kempinski, whom she met on her last visit to Spain and was quite charmed by, will surely have her winging her way southwards.

Sheila Mercier worked for eleven years at the Whitehall Theatre, the name of which will always be synonymous with that of her distinguished brother, Sir Brian Rix. She also worked in repertory all over the country, which is probably where she acquired the stamina to play Annie Sugden for the last twenty years.

Now seventy-three, Sheila has devoted her life to dramatic arts and can look back with some satisfaction on what she has achieved. Apart from a spell in the WAAF during the war, she has known no other job but acting. She has one son, Nigel, and two grandchildren, Michael and David.

JACK SUGDEN

JACK SUGDEN has finally come home to Emmerdale Farm and now runs the farm free from what he considers to be the encumbrance of Joe and his progressive thinking. Jack is opposed to new ideas, and proud of his organically raised sheep.

Romantically he has settled down with Sarah Connolly. She and Jack and young Robert are now the new generation of Sugdens occupying Emmerdale Farm. He proposes to Sarah on each anniversary of his original proposal to her (which she turned down) but still meets with refusal. In 1992, as it was a leap year, Jack felt that the onus should be on Sarah to propose, but she flouted tradition by refusing to comply.

Frank Tate's new holiday village and Joe's involvement are currently causing Jack much concern as he believes that the countryside should be left to country folk.

Clive Hornby is the second actor to play Jack Sugden, having succeeded Andrew Burt after one of the character's absences abroad. Clive joined the Liverpool Playhouse as a stage manager before switching to acting after a spell at stage school. Much theatre work followed, and it was while on the West End stage in Agatha Christie's *Murder at the Vicarage* that he was offered one of Emmerdale's leading roles.

JOE SUGDEN

JOE SUGDEN, once the leading light of Emmerdale Farm, is all for moving with the times. As manager of Frank Tate's holiday village, Joe looks to the future and a new, more lively Beckindale. Frank is a difficult boss as he is always reluctant to hand over the reins to his lieutenants – Joe at the holiday village and Christopher at Tate Haulage – but Joe has enough Sugden stubbornness to see him through.

Still unsettled after the break-up of his marriage to Kate, Joe has turned all his attentions to business, but still keeps a fatherly eye on Kate's children, Mark and Rachel, and a critical eye on the comings and goings at Emmerdale.

Frazer Hines began his career by training at the Majorie Newbury School of Dancing in Harrogate before moving on to the Corona Stage School in London.

Early television appearances include 'Z Cars', 'Coronation Street' and as the kilted Jamie in 'Dr Who'. More recently he has been seen as himself in 'Duty Free', and regularly appears on game shows like 'Give Us a Clue' and 'Countdown'. He has just finished hosting 'Country Challenge'.

Like many of the 'Emmerdale' cast, Frazer enjoys horse-riding, and has ridden several winners on the flat. He is married to former water-ski champion Liz Hobbs.

ROBERT SUGDEN

ROBERT SUGDEN is the youngest Sugden, son of Jack and his wife Pat who died in a car accident in 1986. He is already showing great interest in farming activities and in riding his favourite pony from the pony-trekking stable at Home Farm. He looks like carrying on the true Sugden tradition.

Christopher Smith has spent his entire acting career in 'Emmerdale'. He is now seven years old and coming on very well as an actor. He is also a great prankster, and takes delight in pulling stunts on

Madeleine Howard and Clive Hornby who play his 'Emmerdale' parents.

Christopher, who lives in Bradford, has a sister Polly, aged four, and an older brother, Nicholas, who is nine.

CHRISTOPHER TATE

CHRISTOPHER TATE lives very much in the shadow of his father, who still tends to treat him as a little boy. Now married to Kathy, he has veered away from the Hooray Henry image he once had and is much more considerate of the feelings of others. Kathy has had a lot to do with this change as she left him at one time owing to his often thoughtless attempts to take over her life and encumber her with all the trappings of affluence. Christopher should have recognised in himself the very same trait that makes Frank constantly infuriate him by his annoying attempts to interfere in his son's life with Kathy and in the running of Tate Haulage.

Peter Amory did his theatrical training at the Royal Academy of Dramatic Art before making regular appearances on stage. He has appeared in many highly popular television series including 'Boon', 'Inspector Morse' and 'Gentlemen and Players'.

Peter is twenty-six and joined 'Emmerdale' in 1990.

FRANK TATE

FRANK TATE, who owns Home Farm and its estates, is a self-made man ever on the move to add to his wealth and prestige. He also owns Tate Haulage, which is now run by his son, Christopher.

His newly-opened holiday village, on which he employs Joe Sugden as manager and Mark Hughes as general factotum, could well be the first of his many ambitious plans to develop his interests in Beckindale.

Frank is a reformed alcoholic. Few are aware of his problem; but those who are, and have had first-hand experience of it (like Kim and Dolly Skilbeck), know on what thin ice Frank is treading.

Kim is his second wife and not the mother of his two children, Christopher and Zoë, whose natural mother died of cancer some years ago. Zoë has left Beckindale to be a vet in New Zealand.

Norman Bowler first came to the public eye in the BBC's 'Softly Softly' as DS Harry Hawkins. Latter-day viewers will no doubt remember him as the newspaper editor Sam Benson who had a fling with Nicola Freeman in Central's 'Crossroads'. These are well-remembered roles, but Norman has also appeared in a host of other theatrical productions including *The Caretaker* and *Educating Rita*. He is married and has four children.

KATHY TATE

KATHY TATE is the sister of Nick Bates and has married into money in the shape of Christopher Tate, heir-apparent to the empire of his father, entrepreneur Frank.

Kathy was married young, lost her unborn child from an infection caught from sheep, and was widowed soon after when her first husband, Jackie Merrick, shot himself accidentally while hunting a fox for a £10 bet.

Christopher Tate, who arrived soon after, fell for her in a big way. They came together, parted on account of Chris's overbearing and flashy behaviour, but eventually married in November 1991 after Kathy had had a short romance with the local vicar, Tony Charlton. They now live in Mill Cottage, which Frank Tate bought as a wedding present for the young couple, who were not at all pleased to accept it till Christopher arranged to repay the cost to his father. Now Kathy, despite Christopher's blundering DIY activities, has turned it into a very nice home.

Malandra Burrows first appeared on television at the tender age of six in ITV's 'Junior Showtime'. Three years later she became the youngest winner of 'New Faces'.

Born in Liverpool on 4 November 1965, Malandra attended dancing classes at the age of two. She later attended the Mabel Fletcher Drama School. Her first major television roles were two small parts in 'Brookside'. She joined 'Emmerdale' in 1985.

KIM TATE

KIM TATE married Frank soon after his first wife, Jean, died. She had been his secretary for a short time.

Christopher Tate resented her at one time, believing that Frank had cheated on his first wife to take up with Kim, but recently he has accepted Kim as a truly loving wife to his sometimes difficult father.

Kim's great love is horses, and with new stepdaughter-in-law Kathy she runs a livery stable at Home Farm and a pony-trekking centre set up after she saved a clutch of ponies from the knacker's yard.

When things became difficult in the family business, Kim not only continued to keep the flag flying by breeding and selling thoroughbreds, but also weighed in with the secretarial work and helped to run the office.

She became pregnant after Frank's vasectomy reversal, but kept the news to

herself until after she had been thrown from a horse at the Hotten Show, broke a leg and had a miscarriage.

Neil Kincaid helped out during her indisposition, but their proximity has led to a romantic development bound to end in heartache.

Claire King, who has her own record label, Visual Records, worked as a disc jockey in Leeds and sang in a punk band before she joined 'Emmerdale' – a very far cry from the fashion-conscious lady of Home Farm.

Her blonde hair and blue eyes are the result of having an Irish father and a Scottish mother, but she was born in Yorkshire and therefore 'came home' to Beckindale.

Off duty, Claire enjoys swimming, the cinema and travelling to sunny places. Like Kim Tate she has a love of horses and often rides, attends horse racing and has even ridden as an amateur jockey.

ALAN TURNER

ALAN TURNER holds himself in high esteem and regards himself as almost the unofficial squire of Beckindale. He plays a big part in local affairs as a councillor, as the boss of the trout farm and as owner of the Woolpack.

At the moment he has no romance in his life but still casts his eye fondly in the direction of Caroline Bates, to whom he was once engaged, and takes an over-active interest in the affairs of Elizabeth Feldmann who manages the trout farm for him.

He is a snob *par excellence* and once revelled in his position on the Hunt Committee. He shocked Beckindale – and particularly Henry Wilks – when he took over the Woolpack, gutted it and turned it into an up-market hostelry complete with rural impedimenta (including a mantrap) for décor and a restaurant whose excellence, with Alan as chef, is beyond dispute.

Richard Thorp first became nationally famous as Dr Rennie in 'Emergency – Ward 10' where he rubbed shoulders with John Alderton, Desmond Carrington and Glyn Owen. He stayed with the series throughout its run. Later he appeared in television dramas such as 'Honey Lane', 'Public Eye' and 'Oxbridge 2000', whilst also submitting himself to the indignities which usually befell all those who appeared with Benny Hill and Harry Worth.

As Alan Turner he is a stuffy self-righteous snob; but this is a far cry from the real-life image of Richard, clad in leathers and riding his favourite Harley-Davidson motorbike.

LYNN WHITELEY

LYNN WHITELEY, robbed of her two-timing husband Pete by Kate Sugden's drunken driving, bears up to her widowhood with mixed fortunes.

She currently occupies Whiteley's Farm in the company of baby Peter and Michael Feldmann, who has finally landed romantically on her doorstep after the pair had been attracted to each other for some time. Archie Brooks, who was at one time her lodger, has recently left; but at one time, when her emotional behaviour caused her to pursue both Michael Feldmann and Jack Sugden, he was one of her few friends in Beckindale.

Happily Lynn seems now to be on a steadier course, and could find true happiness with Michael.

Fionnuala Ellwood has two sisters both of whom are in the theatrical profession. One is a stage manager and the other is a theatre administrator.

Fionnuala, who joined 'Emmerdale' in November 1988, might well have been engaged in another soap instead as she took part in the pilot episode of Granada's 'Families'. She also appeared on television in the award-winning 'Prime Suspect'.

She enjoys reading, embroidery and DIY in her spare time, but still finds time for her other two pleasures: cooking and *eating*.

As may be guessed from her name, Fionnuala has an Irish connection, and she was born in Dublin.

HENRY WILKS

HENRY WILKS, a prosperous Bradford mill-owner, took early retirement to Beckindale but proved a very active senior citizen, turning Emmerdale Farm into a thriving enterprise as a limited company and helping Amos to run the Woolpack until his 1991 heart-attack.

Arthur Pentelow was a member of the 'Emmerdale' cast from the very beginning. His other television appearances included 'Z

Cars', 'The Troubleshooters', 'Emergency – Ward 10', 'United' and 'Coronation Street'. He also appeared in several feature films.

❖ L A N D M A R K S ❖

SKIPDALE

SKIPDALE, with a population of some 50,000, is one of the Dales' larger towns, though by no means a major industrial centre. Skipdale Castle, built in the twelfth century by the local Jorvall family, is a renowned landmark; while tourists are also attracted to the Skipdale Commercial Canal, built for barges laden with wool to reach West Yorkshire but now more often covered with canal boats and pleasure-craft. Ephraim Monk's Skipdale Ales are brewed in the town by the only one of fifteen breweries still surviving from the start of the nineteenth century. More modern businesses are accommodated on a trading estate, where Tate Haulage has its base.

HOME FARM

HOME FARM is at the centre of what was for a long time known as the Verney estate. Squire George Verney was the patriarch of the village and surrounding area; but on his death his nephew Gerald, who inherited, was obliged to sell in order to pay death duties.

   The purchasers were NY Estates, and they moved in a succession of managers.

   When NY decided to sell up, Home Farm was bought by former NY employees Alan Turner and Joe Sugden. However, they had great difficulty in making the property pay - and their endeavours were not helped by the scheming of Dennis

Kim and Frank Tate, the current owner/occupiers of Home Farm (opposite).

Rigg, whose company had plans to turn the whole area into a quarry. These plans foundered when Rigg was accidentally crushed by Joe's prize bull.

Home Farm was then bought by Frank Tate. He is by no means farming-orientated, and is happy to take government money to let much of Home Farm lie idle under EC regulations to avoid over-supply.

While young second wife Kim is running a successful stables, Frank Tate is none too fond of the hunt - though Home Farm has hosted the hunt ball on occasion. The fish farm, which rears trout in tanks for the restaurant trade, has been under Alan Turner's control since the summer of 1989, and he runs it with assistance from Elizabeth Feldmann and rather less help from Seth Armstrong. He also runs a shoot.

HOME FARM

The Lady Mayoress of Hotten opens the Home Farm holiday village, with Frank and Kim Tate in attendance.

The biggest change to Home Farm came with the 1992 opening of the holiday village, Frank Tate's brainchild, which he has brought Joe Sugden in to manage. Opposition from Jack to an influx of 'townies' is significant, though a school of thought – led by Alan Turner – believes it could bring prosperity to Beckindale, too.

The Sugden Perspective

They play mother and son Annie and Joe Sugden as if born to the relationship, yet twenty years ago neither Sheila Mercier nor Frazer Hines had the slightest inkling they would still be playing their respective roles in 'Emmerdale' today.

'They asked me about the thirteen episodes – or thirteen weeks,' Sheila recalls, 'and then they said: "Would you be willing to stay for two years?" I talked to my family about it, and we decided I would. I think I was the only one they mentioned two years to.'

'I can remember as if it were yesterday', recalls Frazer, 'that our production assistant came into the canteen one day during a tea-break and said: "I've just seen a script for episode twenty-six." We all thought: Another thirteen episodes – wonderful. At the end of episode nine my character had a car crash, and Annie had to say: "It's the hospital. Joe's not expected to live." I couldn't wait to get episode ten's script …'

Frazer took three years off in the mid-eighties to recharge his batteries: conveniently Joe Sugden went to work for NY Estates in France. Yet he has no regrets about returning. 'People have said to me: "How can you stay in something for so *long*?" The answer is it's great fun to do – still. And time goes by so quickly. You go on holiday in the summer, and then it's Christmas… Before you know where you are, they're saying: "Do you want to stay for *another* year?"

'It concertinas,' agrees Sheila. 'You think that something's happened last year and it happened five years ago. You're not aware of the passing of time. It's extraordinary.'

In the early days, the actors had yet to find home bases near the Leeds studios, and there was a fair amount of travelling involved. 'It was very hard work,' recalls

A family united: Joe (Frazer Hines), Annie (Sheila Mercier) and Jack Sugden (Clive Hornby).

Sheila Mercier and Frazer Hines in the Farmhouse kitchen – scene of so much 'Emmerdale' action – with Malandra Burrows (Kathy).

Sheila. 'We rehearsed on Sundays in those days. I used to go down at the weekend – drive myself in those days – and at the end of a year I wondered why I was having twitches. I used to share with Freddie Pyne an awful lot. He used to pick me up at seven o'clock in the morning at Waterloo Station, and off we'd go. But I stopped driving eventually and went by train, because it was just *too* stressful.'

'I used to drive on a Friday night all the way down to near Gatwick Airport,' Frazer remembers, 'and thought nothing of driving straight up to location on Monday morning.'

In the beginning, Sheila remembers, mother and son were on camera almost all the time. 'We had an awful lot to do, because there were only about eight of us and we were in all the time. There were a couple of episodes when, I think, I was hardly off the screen at all.'

Life should be easier now; but, as the cast has grown, so the frequency has increased. With 'Emmerdale' on television all year round, Frazer concedes that normal life is bound to suffer. 'In a way,' he admits, 'it was nicer when we were a series, when we used to come off in the summer for about three months, because then you could actually do other things or just do nothing if you wanted to. Then we became a twice-weekly soap …'

The consistently high standard of 'Emmerdale' is something Frazer and Sheila are proud of. Yet, as Frazer explains, there have inevitably been changes over the twenty years.

'When you start a series it can be grittier, earthier, slower-moving, because it was only meant to run thirteen or fourteen episodes. You can't have that now in a twice-weekly soap opera, because people would be making the tea or switching off. I'm pleased that it *has* kept to a certain standard. Obviously the first writers had the best ideas. If Dickens were still writing, even *he* would be running out of ideas by now!'

Sheila pinpoints one major difference. 'The thing that's changed enormously is that there are far more young people in it now. It was written around middle-aged and older people; now it's a lot of young people. Then, our characters have changed a lot; they're *bound* to have. Joe grew up, for one thing …'

Frazer: 'Yes, I was quite fortunate, because Joe started off eighteen and not married and got married and divorced and a second wife, whereas if I'd been

A somewhat younger Joe Sugden. Frazer has been with the series from the beginning, barring a three year break.

playing Amos at fifty there's a great deal of the character set.'

The Woolpack's bewhiskered landlord is now, of course, part of 'Emmerdale' history, having left for Spain – where Annie Sugden visits him. Of the regular characters of yesteryear, Amos Brearly (Ronald Magill) and his fellow-host, Henry Wilks (the late Arthur Pentelow), are the characters Frazer and Sheila miss the most, while Freddie Pyne – who played Matt Skilbeck from the beginning to 1989 – is a close personal friend of both of them.

Three generations of farming folk: Sam Pearson (Toke Townley, second left), Annie Sugden and son Joe, with son-in-law Matt Skilbeck (Freddie Pyne, left).

'Ronnie and Arthur *are* missed,' muses Frazer. 'And Toke [Townley, who played Sam Pearson] – mustn't forget him, because the character he played was great. We haven't got that old character in the show. That's one character the show needs – the grumpy old grandad. He brought in a lot of traditions like the Beckstone Thrash and the First World War reunions and the idea of the memorial services. Obviously, if you lose a character like that, young people don't want to remember the Great War or beating the bounds, so we lost a lot of tradition when the grandfather figure died.'

'I used to have an awful lot of scenes with Toke,' adds Sheila, 'and when he went my character practically *halved*, because all the scenes I used to have with him weren't there any more. I'm as old now as Toke was in the beginning.'

Opposite: *Joe's first marriage to Christine Sharp in 1974, which sadly ended in divorce.*

'He was always full of life for his age,' Frazer points out. 'One day I said to him: "You're full of beans today. I bet you can't tap-dance." And he jumped on the table and did a tap-dance! I suppose out of all of them I miss working with him, because sometimes he would be infuriating.

'You'd just get over your worst speech that took you hours to learn, and Toke's line would come up and he'd forget it, and you had to go back to the beginning of the scene again!'

In the twenty years he has played Joe Sugden, Frazer can recall being presented with only one situation he felt by instinct did not ring true. When Joe got married the first time, he was originally going to marry someone else completely. 'There'd been a long relationship building up, the characters getting to know each other, and everything was fine. Then the actress, for some reason we still don't know, didn't come back to the show, and according to the script Joe's wedding was in twelve weeks' time. So instead of having her run off and leave him at the altar, or whatever, they just went ahead. We had a wedding booked, and I think they wanted the publicity in the newspapers – a soap wedding – so they brought in this girl, Christine Sharp, who'd been in one episode as a Milk Marketing Board representative. Joe married her after about twelve weeks, and I thought at the time that that was totally wrong – just to marry for the sake of the script.'

Like Frazer, Sheila can remember only one unlikely situation she had to portray. 'Annie got hooked on Valium, and she went through an awful lot to get off it. Henry threw her pills away, and the

doctor ticked him off for this because you *never* do it like that.'

As Frazer recalls with that characteristic twinkle in his eye, there have been many moments over the twenty years that have been memorable – and sometimes for the wrong reasons. 'One that springs to mind was a day when the sun was shining but it was very, very windy. We were all sitting out in deckchairs having a cup of tea – Matt, Joe and Annie – and Sheila brought this tray of biscuits and tea out. I got a spoonful of sugar to put in my tea, and the wind just went *whoof!* and blew all the sugar off my spoon. We laughed like *drains* …

'I can't think of any really *horrible* moments. Freddie would probably say when he was pot-holing. That must have been awful for him, because when they were filming he actually had to go down in a pot-hole. They were lucky he didn't have claustrophobia!'

'I couldn't have done it,' shudders Sheila. 'Nothing on *earth* would have got me down there!'

When 'Emmerdale' started, working with animals was a major part of the job description for any prospective cast-member. Consequently, Sheila and Frazer are both very much at home on the farm. Nevertheless, some things take a bit of getting used to, as Sheila recalls. 'I was feeding the cows once, and as I walked back between them they moved together and squashed the bucket I was carrying. A second later, and it would have been *me* that was squashed!'

Neither believes that being Yorkshire-born (as they both are) is a necessary qualification for surviving twenty years of 'Emmerdale'. Sports fanatic Frazer admits he would have loved to play for the county cricket team; yet in the first-ever cricket match in 'Emmerdale' Matt, not Joe, was cast as the demon bowler. 'Now they've got the message, and they wrote Joe in the next time we had a cricket match. Joe was the one who hit the winning six and took three wickets, because I play cricket.

'It's a good idea', Frazer continues, 'for writers to pick up on people's hobbies and write it in that the character actually does that. You don't go down to the writers or the producer and say: "Wouldn't it be a good idea if Joe did this or Annie did this?" I think they actually pick it up themselves. They know that I horse-ride, and they know that Claire King horse-rides, so it'd be silly not to bring that in. It's no good writing a character horse-rides if that actress can't. Little Leah

*Matt Skilbeck goes down the pot-hole to rescue
a Scandinavian tourist in 1977.*

Frazer Hines and Claire King (Kim Tate) are both keen horse-riders and happily saddle-up for the cameras.

[Bracknell, who played Zoë Tate] wasn't very fond of horses, and that's why she stopped – because she was doing a lot of riding and just didn't like it. I think the first horse she rode was a bit skittery, and that put her off.'

As well as its unpredictable horses, Yorkshire is also known for its deceptive climate. As with the sugar episode, what looks sunny on screen may actually be freezing in the flesh. 'I think some of the worst times', Sheila recalls, 'have been in the summer-time on outside broadcast when you're in summer dresses and the cold is absolutely like a knife. It's bad enough in the winter when it's cold, but in the summer when it's cold you can't wear thermals with summer dresses!'

'It looks like you're in the middle of Spain,' agrees Frazer, 'but outside it could be really freezing. So if you're wearing a big thick anorak viewers will write in

Sheila submits to the make-up brush before a day's shooting.

and say: "Why were Joe and Annie wearing big thick coats?" '

'OB can be absolute *murder* on your figure,' Sheila explains, 'because you go out there and there'll be bacon butties first thing. Then you have this enormous lunch, then tea, sandwiches and cakes. You can eat your way through the day, and at the end of two or three days' filming you're half a stone heavier! It's very difficult to resist that smell of bacon when it's wafting in the air.'

Talking of food, the Emmerdale kitchen has been the centre of so much of the action over two decades. Not a lot has changed, though it did have a revamp after eighteen years or so. 'More recently than that,' Sheila reveals, 'they put in a new Aga that doesn't even work! At least the old Aga worked, but this one doesn't. You can't fry bacon and eggs like you used to, because there's no heat coming from it.'

Joe is supposed to be a bit of a cook, but Frazer confesses that's the one thing he *really* has to act. 'When Joe was preparing chicken in Calvados, I think that probably showed, because I think a person that cooks has a natural flair for preparing stuff. In the end we used a whole bottle of Calvados, because they wanted to see the flames.'

With the emphasis now rather less on farming, Frazer and Sheila are keeping a watchful eye on the 'rural aspect', as Frazer calls it. 'I think if they lose any more', he warns, 'it'll become like "Neighbours". The biggest single factor in the continuing popularity of "Emmerdale" is, simply, fresh air – the countryside, the outdoors. I think if we'd just been set in the farm kitchen and in the pub it wouldn't have lasted. I think it's the outdoors, the village life.'

Though he claims to have no regrets at his twenty-year stay on the farm, Frazer admits to one secret unfulfilled ambition. Had he not been in 'Emmerdale', there's another soap he would love to have played a part in. ' "Dallas". I would love to have done something like that. I'd have played JR: he was one of those people that you *love* to hate.'

'But he was stuck in an office all the time,' Sheila disagrees. 'You'd have *hated* that.'

'Well, how about the ranch-hand, then – Ray Krebbs?' Frazer compromises. And quite right, too. After all, Mother knows best!

THE WOOLPACK

THE WOOLPACK is the foremost of Beckindale's two licensed hostelries. (The other is the Malt Shovel.)

The present-day Woolpack is in fact the second pub of that name: the first Woolpack inn was declared dangerous owing to subsidence in 1976, and a corn chandler's dwelling was taken over and converted into a two-bar establishment. This newer hostelry even survived a gas explosion in 1984. Ruling the roost through these and many other incidents was Amos Brearly, landlord since the end of the war, who latterly presided with former mill-owner Henry Wilks, whose money had helped buy the freehold when Ephraim Monk's brewery wanted to sell it off.

The arrival of Alan Turner as 'mine host' in 1991 after Amos Brearly's retirement to sunnier climes has seen a greater emphasis on food. He has turned the tap room – formerly used as a family room at lunchtimes and a young people's meeting-place at night – into a restaurant.

The main bar where the locals congregate is where most of the action takes place. There is an adjoining back room which serves as an office. There is also a cellar, which has in the past been plagued by rats: Seth Armstrong was once persuaded to spend a night down there with Pete Whiteley in an attempt to eradicate the pests. If Alan Turner is to be believed, Seth is one pest the Woolpack has yet to get rid of!

Woolpack landlord, Alan Turner.

Year by Year

1972

The death of Jacob Sugden in October threw Emmerdale into turmoil; for, by bequeathing the farm to Jack, his elder son, the head of the family simultaneously alienated Joe, his other son, who had been the obvious choice to step into his father's shoes. Joe had worked with brother-in-law Matt Skilbeck to keep the farm afloat after Jacob had turned to drink. Now the prospect of his elder brother returning to the fold as his

Sam, Annie, Jack, Peggy, Matt and Joe: a family mourns.

father's appointed heir seemed certain to cause a family rift.

Surprisingly, the answer came from outside the Sugden hierarchy – from Henry Wilks, a former mill-owner who had recently retired to Inglebrook, a large house situated next to Emmerdale. The Sugdens had not immediately taken to their new neighbour, who had wasted no time in making his presence felt with a row over the right of way, but Jack Sugden had eyes for Henry's daughter, Marian. Henry's objective in purchasing the head lease of Emmerdale and suggesting a partnership between Jack, himself and the rest of the family was to provide for his daughter's future. The romance between Jack and Marian was not to last; but Emmerdale's future was secure, thanks to Henry's money and a share scheme defining the Sugdens' various responsibilities.

Though Jack was temporarily ensnared, he put a little distance between himself and the rest of the family by converting a disused watermill on Emmerdale land into living accommodation, with help from a friend who came up from London. There was certainly little room to spare at Emmerdale itself: sister Peggy and her husband, Matt Skilbeck, a quiet yet hard-working labourer, were expecting twins – to provide Annie Sugden with her first grandchildren and her father, Sam Pearson, with great-grandchildren.

1973

Peggy Skilbeck gave birth to twins Sam and Sally in February, timing them to arrive in the peace and quiet just before the start of the lambing season. She and Matt moved to the farmhouse at Jamieson's, a smallholding between Jack's mill and Inglebrook, intended for development as holiday cottages but now rechristened Hawthorn Cottage.

Inglebrook, meanwhile, burned down in a mystery blaze, and Henry Wilks was forced to seek temporary lodging at Emmerdale. Uncomfortable under the Sugdens' roof, he decided to ask Amos Brearly if he could rent a room at the Woolpack as a short-term measure – destined to last some seventeen years! Down at the mill, Jack had abandoned his attempts at conversion and had befriended a local tramp, nicknamed Trash, who had taken up residence with him.

When Ephraim Monk's brewery suddenly put the Woolpack up for sale, the village rallied round to save it. Henry Wilks proved Amos's most potent weapon, putting up the money to ensure that the pub retained both its landlord and its traditional character, and a mass desertion to the rival Malt Shovel was averted.

The first Beckindale wedding was seen in March when Janie Harker married blacksmith Frank Blakey. Jack Sugden was best man, and the ceremony was performed by the Reverend Edward Ruskin.

Peggy Skilbeck's unexpected death when a blood vessel burst in her brain occurred when the twins were just three months old, and she was buried alongside her father in the village churchyard in May. Widower Matt threw himself back into his work, while the twins went to live at nearby Blackfell with his Aunt Beattie. While driving with the twins one day, her car stalled at a level crossing and was struck by a train, killing all the occupants outright – a stunning triple tragedy that made 1973 memorable for all the wrong reasons.

1974

As the year began, Jack Sugden left the mill to move to Rome – where the globe-trotting Marian Wilks had now ended up – to write the script for a film of his best-selling novel *Field of Tares*.

Joe Sugden, meanwhile, became involved with Christine Sharp, an employee of the Milk Marketing Board, and after a whirlwind courtship their engagement was announced. Her father, a wealthy landowner, did not think that Joe was good enough for Christine and strongly disapproved of their intended union. The marriage went ahead never-theless, with Henry Wilks deputising for the bride's absent father. (Sam Pearson had been the original choice but refused to wear morning dress.)

The first cracks in the new marriage were soon to show after the couple returned from their London honeymoon and moved into Hawthorn Cottage where Matt and Peggy had lived. Joe's disap-proval of her refurnishing the house with her father's money proved the last straw; and Christine roared out of Beckindale in her sports-car, vowing never to return.

Back at the farm, a traveller called

Christine Sharp, who became the first and short-lived Mrs Joe Sugden in 1974.

King of the road, Dryden Hogben.

Dryden Hogben was discovered camping on Emmerdale land, and was promptly befriended by the Sugdens. He was something of a handyman, so they employed him to convert the farmhouse attic into the bedroom it remains to this day.

1975

When Jean Kendall, Annie's cousin, had to go into hospital for a long stay, she was naturally concerned for her two children, Rosemary and Peter. Rosemary, aged seventeen, came to live at Emmerdale and soon became a particular favourite of Sam Pearson, whose grandchildren had now flown the nest.

Down at the Woolpack, landlord Amos Brearly nearly fell victim to a widow living outside Hotten who decided that she needed a 'new' husband. Appalled, Amos declined her proposal of marriage and resumed his bachelor life with some relief.

Annie had a busy year, becoming a churchwarden and learning to drive, relying more and more on Rosemary's help to keep the farm running in her absence.

1976

Amos got the job of Beckindale correspondent for the *Hotten Courier* and had to suffer a visit from his Aunt Emily. More serious problems arose when the Woolpack suffered structural damage and was forced to move to an entirely new location at the other end of Beckindale. He nearly called off the move because the new building (the

Publican Amos Brearly's 'other job': writing for the local paper.

present Woolpack) was supposedly haunted, but common sense in the shape of Henry Wilks prevailed and the relocation was finally completed without undue difficulty.

Another forced move in prospect was that of Nellie Dawson, an old flame of Sam Pearson. She turned down his belated proposal of marriage, but was happy when he led the fight to save her cottage when NY Estates tried to evict her.

The Gimbel family, who lived at

neighbouring Holly Farm, entered the Sugdens' life when Joe befriended daughter Kathy and Rosemary started to date Kathy's brother, Martin.

Both recovering from unhappy marriages, Joe and Kathy sought solace in each other's company, their friendship quickly growing to love. Martin, however, left to join the Army after a final confrontation with his overbearing father, Jim.

The autumn saw the return of two of Emmerdale's black sheep: Jack Sugden and Christine Sharp. Though welcomed at first, Christine's belated attempt to patch up her marriage foundered on Joe's affection for Kathy

Gimbel. The return of his estranged wife made Joe recognise his true feelings, and he finally rejected Christine's overtures, deciding instead to file for divorce. Rosemary, who had secretly fallen in love with Joe herself, was understandably heartbroken and left the farm to live with her now-recovered mother in Middlesbrough.

Christine's father attempted to get half of Joe's share in Emmerdale for his daughter as part of the divorce settlement, but Henry Wilks came to the rescue by suggesting that Joe claim half of the Sharp dairy farm. Needless to say, the matter was never raised again.

1977

His mind now made up, Joe Sugden sold Hawthorn Cottage along with its bad memories and bought the cottage at 3 Demdyke Row, and a village scandal erupted when he set up home there with Kathy Gimbel. They could not marry because each was awaiting a divorce, but public opinion overlooked this and the fact that both marriages were effectively over before the couple even met.

A new face greeted customers at the Woolpack as Dolly Acaster took on the role of barmaid. She could not claim to come from a farming background, but was seconded to work in the Woolpack as part of a training scheme run by Ephraim Monk's brewery. Dolly left Beckindale when Amos was particularly uncooperative, but Henry Wilks re-employed her later in the year.

At St Mary's Church there was another new arrival in the shape of the Reverend William Hockley, the long-overdue – if temporary – replacement for the Reverend Edward Ruskin.

A Swedish couple, Asta and Olof Gunnarson, stayed at the Woolpack, which was taking in bed-and-breakfast guests, but went pot-holing and got trapped in Baker's Pot. Matt Skilbeck led the rescue team.

Up at Holly Farm, Jim Gimbel could not cope with the fact that Kathy was living with Joe Sugden. Left alone when his wife Freda followed his son and daughter and left, he shot himself dead – with the result that Kathy, riddled with guilt, left Joe and moved to Hotten.

Annie Sugden and Sam Pearson enjoyed their first-ever holiday abroad when they went to visit Jack in Italy. In their absence, Matt's girlfriend, Lucy Stubbs, stayed at the farm; but when she left Dolly Acaster became involved with Matt – a relationship that was clearly destined to end in marriage.

A second new arrival at St Mary's in a year, the Reverend David Cowper was replaced by the Reverend Donald Hinton, who would prove Beckindale's longest-serving vicar, retiring in 1989.

Pat Merrick's brother, Syd Harker, and her husband, Tom, poached sheep from Emmerdale to sell as meat to a butcher in Hotten. (Tom Merrick was still fuming about being sacked from Emmerdale in 1974.) Syd then broke into Demdyke, but PC Edwards arrested him, bringing Beckindale's miniature crime-wave to a timely end.

1978

Crime reared its head in Beckindale once more when local teenagers Steve Hawker and Pip Coulter robbed the Woolpack, and locked Amos and Henry in the cellar overnight. When pursued by the police, they fled to Emmerdale and held Sam Pearson at gunpoint. Annie's clear head saved the day: she gave them a car to escape in, in order both to save Sam and to disarm them.

More guns were in the news after Clive Hinton visited his clergyman father and was subsequently arrested in Athens for gun-running.

Seth Armstrong made his first appearance in May as the school caretaker. New teacher Anthony Moeketsi discovered that Seth could not read and taught him. Meanwhile Seth's son Fred managed to give Amos chicken pox, and the bewhiskered landlord had to move into Emmerdale to recuperate.

Richard Roper, Dolly Acaster's former boyfriend and the father of her ille-gitimate son, arrived in Beckindale. He attempted to win her back, their earlier relationship having been ended by his disapproving mother; but Dolly proceeded with her plans and married Matt in June.

The Home Farm estate was sold by Gerald Verney and his wife Charlotte to pay death duties following the death of his Uncle George, the former squire of Beckindale. NY Estates bought the property and sent Trevor Thatcher and his wife Paula to manage it. Trevor started off on the wrong foot, immediately arresting Sam Pearson for poaching pheasants – not realising that the actual culprit was Seth! Maurice Westrop arrived as the new manager later in the year.

Marian Wilks returned to visit her father and try to persuade him to move to Italy. He contemplated selling his share in the Woolpack to his old army-officer friend Major Denyer, but finally decided to stay after all.

1979

Having survived the previous year's scare that Henry might leave the Woolpack for good, Amos was afraid that history was repeating itself when Henry became involved with Irene Madden, a widow who had moved in next door to Joe Sugden in Demdyke Row. Romance cooled, however, and Henry and Irene remained just good friends – much to Amos's barely concealed relief and delight.

Local ne'er-do-well Phil Fletcher was accidentally shot in the leg during an argument with Joe Sugden over shooting rights on Emmerdale land. Phil owed Emmerdale money and forced his son, Terry, to lie to the police, accusing Joe of doing it deliberately.

Over at Home Farm, Maurice Westrop hired Seth Armstrong as gamekeeper for NY Estates possibly on the basis that a poacher was the best man for the job. Less happily, his daughter Judy arrived in town suffering from acute depression after an abortion.

Ed Hathersage and land agent Geoff Atwill tried to open a farm museum on land next to Emmerdale; despite much effort, the project failed. Up at the farm, delight was the order of the day when Dolly discovered that she was pregnant.

1980

The departure of Home Farm manager Maurice Westrop, who was transferred to North Wales, had dramatic repercussions outside farm boundaries. His replacement, the dynamic Richard Anstey, persuaded Joe Sugden to leave Emmerdale and become assistant manager at Home Farm.

The upheaval this caused at Emmerdale was matched by events at the Woolpack when Henry's Cousin Alice and Amos's Aunt Emily arrived to stay – at the same time!

Pat Merrick was back in town with children Jackie and Sandie, having divorced husband Tom for persistent physical and mental abuse. She moved in with her Aunt Elsie and took a job as a waitress at Hotten Market café to make ends meet.

Jackie befriended Seth Armstrong, who gave him a Saturday job as gamekeeper's assistant. Pat's return was greeted with more than usual interest by Jack Sugden, now once again resident at Emmerdale. They had been having a teenage affair when he left Beckindale to become a bestselling author in the capital, and the spark of love had never entirely died. Now free of Marian Wilks, Jack was keen to fan the embers of that earlier relationship and see what resulted.

Dolly miscarried Matt's baby after eight months and was lucky to survive the ordeal. After much rest and thought, she decided that life must go on and joined the staff of the local playgroup.

No longer an expectant mother, Dolly becomes a playgroup helper.

1981

Jack Sugden's fast-flourishing relationship with Pat Merrick proved to have aroused opposition, not only from ex-husband Tom, who became involved in a fight with his rival outside the Woolpack, but also from son Jackie, who at first had no idea that the stranger courting his mother was in fact his natural father. Jackie reacted badly to the whole affair, and was accused by Sergeant MacArthur of a series of burglaries in the area. Indeed, burglars had paid

Joe (right) welcomes new boss Alan Turner to Home Farm in 1982.

Emmerdale a visit in April; but more serious was the news in that same month that Jack's prized cattle herd had salmonella and would have to be slaughtered.

When cantankerous local farmer Enoch Tolly died in a tractor accident, Seth Armstrong, the garrulous gamekeeper, was on hand to help out. He persuaded the late farmer's wife, Grace, to employ Daniel Hawkins, who had just resigned from NY Estates. (He would return to Home Farm the following year when Grace was forced to sell up.)

Elsewhere on the employment front, Dolly had started work at the playgroup, while Pat Merrick became housekeeper for the Reverend Donald Hinton at St Mary's vicarage.

Richard Anstey had an affair with Virginia Lattimore, wife of the regional manager of NY Estates, and was predictably sacked when the relationship came to light. Joe Sugden was asked to fill in until a new estate manager could be found.

The year ended less than festively for the light-fingered Tom Merrick, who received a suspended sentence for stealing Christmas trees!

1982

Alan Turner arrived as the new man in charge of Home Farm, but immediately found himself in difficulties. Reconciling the orders of head office with the practicalities of running a country estate efficiently and profitably was no easy task. One of his first moves was to try to lure Matt Skilbeck to NY Estates, using the old Tolly farmhouse he had recently acquired as bait. Turner's ploy was unsuccessful, while Jack's ire was aroused in May when

Dolly welcomes long-awaited offspring, Samuel David to the Skilbeck family.

careless crop-spraying caused his cattle to stampede.

After her miscarriage – not to mention Matt's earlier tragedies – everyone was delighted when Dolly produced a fine son, Samuel David. The proud parents had intended to call him David Samuel, but grandfather Sam had got the wrong end of the stick and, rather than upset him, they decided to reverse the names.

Dolly's labour had not been without its share of drama: Jackie Merrick drove her to hospital even though he did not have a driving licence. Once peace had

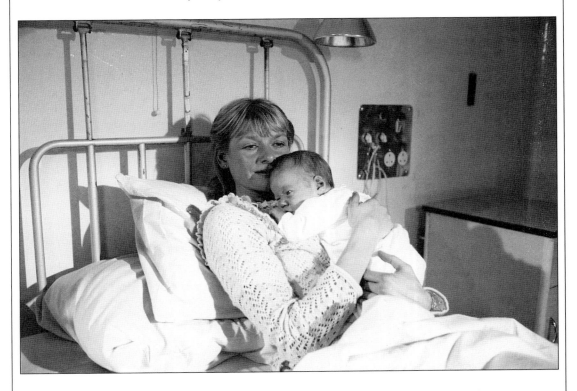

been restored, Matt and Dolly moved into a two-bedroom extension cottage at Emmerdale despite competition from Jack. But Dolly continued to dream of a home of her own.

The Reverend Donald Hinton, who had by now become rural dean, refused to marry Jack and Pat because Pat was a divorcée. Undeterred, the couple were married in Hotten register office in October after a turbulent year in which Jackie, the couple's child from their earlier relationship, had simply found it impossible to accept his natural father. What was worse, Tom Merrick – the man he had grown up believing was his father and whose surname he shared – ostracised him. Jackie's reaction was to get drunk and go poaching. He left Emmerdale and returned to a caravan the family had previously rented from NY Estates, then set fire to it after his employer, NY boss Alan Turner, sacked him for making a hash of a shooting party. He was later arrested and moved into the vicarage. His conviction for arson (he received 120 hours' community service) gave him a criminal record which stopped him from fulfilling a boyhood dream of joining the Army, but was ironically to prove a turning-point in his life.

1983

The Beckindale economy hit a new low this year. At Emmerdale, Annie insisted that Henry Wilks take over the accounts when the farm hit financial trouble; while over at Home Farm severe cutbacks were being made and 50 per cent redundancies threatened.

Joe Sugden left Beckindale in October for a new NY Estates post in France after his relationship with the Reverend Donald Hinton's daughter Barbara Peters fell apart.

Donald Hinton and daughter Barbara discuss her affair with Joe.

Barbara, who had left her husband, worked at Home Farm as Alan Turner's secretary and had been carrying on the affair despite the ill-concealed disapproval of her father. The month of Joe's departure saw Beckindale's chances of winning the Best Kept Village competition disappear when a cartload of horse manure was dumped in the Woolpack car park.

The Woolpack's most celebrated patron, Seth Armstrong, was not smelling of roses, either. His long-suffering wife, Meg, finally threw him out because of his excessive drinking – and it took all the diplomatic skill of the Reverend Edward Ruskin, filling in while Donald Hinton was away, to bring about a reconciliation.

Sandie Merrick, meanwhile, was expecting a child. She would not name the father, who turned out to be student Andy Longthorn, a former schoolmate and the son of a local farmer. He left Beckindale for university. In his absence Sandie understandably looked for support, which came not from her mother but from Dolly Skilbeck. Sandie decided to have the baby, and went up to Aberdeen (where Tom Merrick was working on the oil-rigs) for the later months of her pregnancy.

1984

Caroline Bates started as NY Estates secretary in February – the latest in a long line of assistants for Alan Turner. Many had come and gone, unable to tolerate his drinking, gambling and amorous intent, but Mrs Bates was made of sterner stuff.

Turner himself could well have been on the job market, having been threatened with dismissal by Christopher Meadows for drinking and gambling excessively. In an effort to turn over a new leaf, Turner planned a reconciliation with estranged wife Jill, who had started by selecting his new secretary.

Sandie decided to have her daughter adopted and returned to Emmerdale, initially with her father. She had survived despite a notable lack of sympathy from her mother, who – it was widely noted – had not visited her in Aberdeen before her confinement. In the end, Sandie joined the extended family at Emmerdale, where Sam Pearson was particularly taken with her. At length, she and Pat were reconciled, and she found a new career for herself at Hotten Market, where she would rise to the heights of auctioneer.

Elsewhere, Jackie Merrick blamed gamekeeper Seth Armstrong when his father, Derek Warner and Kevin Haynes were arrested for poaching fish. As Jack Sugden's old flame Marian Wilks married in Italy, he started an affair with Hotten Market secretary Karen Moore which would only end with an ultimatum from wife Pat: come home or lose her for ever.

Someone else who returned home – if only temporarily – was Joe Sugden, back at Emmerdale for Christmas. But one familiar face was missing from the festive table. Sam Pearson had died peacefully in his sleep in November, his body discovered by dutiful daughter Annie when she took him his morning cup of tea. The previous night had been spent celebrating his pumpkin winning first prize in the village's annual show; so at least Sam went out in style.

1985

The annual Beckindale village fête was enlivened this year when Seth Armstrong's donkey ran amok. Fortunately, he was still able to retreat to the Woolpack for a reviving pint since the Malt Shovel's barmaid, Doreen, was persuaded to help out there behind the bar while Henry was in Italy with his daughter.

Seth was unlucky all round, losing out to Alan Turner – of all people – in an election for the parish council. Turner's hoped-for reconciliation with Jill ended in disappointment and divorce, though he had the dubious consolation of the company of their son, Terence, who moved to Beckindale after he was thrown out of Oxford University and promptly became involved with Sandie Merrick, who was witness to local quarry-owner

Jackie Merrick is taken to hospital after being hit by Alan Turner's car.

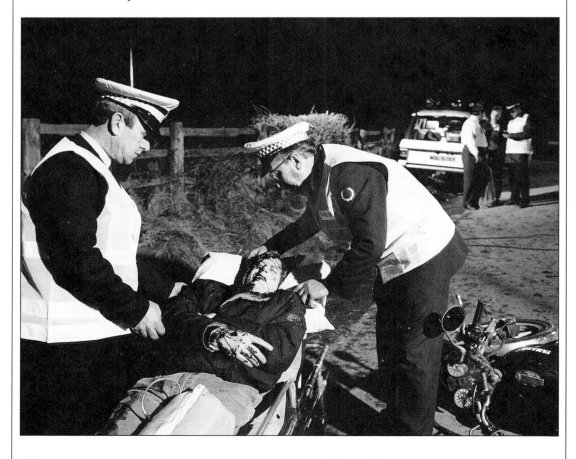

Matt Skilbeck and Harry Mowlem come to blows: the quarry-owner would meet a violent death in 1986.

Harry Mowlem and petty criminal Derek Warner robbing a security van of £6,000.

Jackie Merrick and Alison Caswell had started to go out together the previous year, but they broke up when she felt he had started to take her for granted. He bought a new motorbike to ease his disappointment, but was accidentally knocked down in a dark country lane by Alan Turner's vehicle. He spent the following five months recovering in hospital, where he met and fell in love with nurse Sita Sharma. Having become reconciled with Jack during the first desperate days when his life hung in the balance – for the first time he even called him 'Dad' – Jackie returned to Emmerdale a wiser young man.

Sita and Jackie subsequently became engaged, but she ended the liaison after Jackie started to pressurise her. Another relationship to end this year was that of Caroline Bates and husband Malcolm, who was having an affair.

Harry Mowlem, who had bought thirty acres adjoining Emmerdale to raise pigs and cause trouble, made improper advances to pregnant Dolly, who shortly afterwards miscarried.

1986

This was a year of births, marriages and deaths. Away from Beckindale, in March future Home Farm owner Frank Tate was marrying second wife Kim; while, closer to home, Robert Sugden was born to proud parents Jack and Pat. Tragedy struck just five months later, however, when Pat swerved to avoid a flock of sheep, her car left the road and she was killed.

The village scandal of the year was another death: that of Harry Mowlem. Matt Skilbeck was in the frame thanks to a widely witnessed disagreement between the two men over Mowlem's alleged sheep-stealing that had earlier led to blows. The £6,000 from the previous year's security-van robbery was found in Mowlem's pig-shelter. Matt's innocence was established beyond doubt when Mowlem's associate Derek Warner confessed to murdering him after a row over the money – but not before holding Donald Hinton hostage in the vicarage in an attempt to get away.

Joe Sugden returned from France to become regional manager of NY Estates – over the head of his former boss, Alan Turner. He bought Hotten Market on behalf of NY Estates, but Eric Pollard – the man appointed to run it – took a dislike to Sandie, and friction developed between them.

If her professional life was fraught, Sandie could at least take comfort from the fact that she now had a steady boyfriend in Phil Pearce. She had been forced to leave Emmerdale by Annie's disapproval of her affair with the married builder, who left wife Lesley to move into the mill with Sandie.

Elsewhere, the Longthorns were evicted from Lower Hall Farm and moved to Lincoln. Jackie Merrick started to date Caroline Bates's daughter, Kathy – the latest, so it seemed, in a long line of lady friends. Joe formed Phoenix Developments with Phil Pearce (their first project having been the mill renovation), while Seth Armstrong was

Local builder Phil Pearce, who set up home with Sandie Merrick during 1986.

Dolly comforts her son, army deserter Graham Lodsworth.

badly beaten by badger-baiters.

Dolly Skilbeck's past came back to haunt her at Christmas in the shape of Graham Lodsworth, her illegitimate son who had deserted from the Army in an attempt to track down his natural mother. He had lived rough in the woods and even destroyed his own car before a burly sergeant-major came to return him to the ranks.

1987

Storm clouds were gathering on the Beckindale horizon with a prospect of having a nuclear dump on their doorstep. A protest meeting was held at the Woolpack with television cameras present, and it was immediately apparent that ever-idealistic Jack Sugden would be the man to lead the protest. With a new

Beckindale's residents gather in protest at Jack's imprisonment.

young son's life to protect, he rode in on his white charger – and was promptly imprisoned for contempt of court! Happily, the plans for the dump were abandoned.

Having enraged Jack by dating his brother's old flame Karen Moore, Joe was now romancing vet Ruth Pennington. It was a relationship that seemed to stand as good a chance as any of ending at the altar. Unfortunately, she was unable to decide between Joe and her former fiancé, a racehorse-breeder named Liam, and left in July the following year.

Sandie told Joe of her suspicions that Eric Pollard was stealing from the market. When the accusations were proved,

Pollard was sacked and started a hate campaign against Sandie, which reached a peak when he broke into the mill and threatened her with a poker.

Marian Wilks returned for a visit with her husband Paolo Rossetti and baby Niccolo. Eric Pollard burgled their house, but was disturbed by Paolo, who pursued him into the woods brandishing a revolver. Unfortunately he tripped and shot himself. While Paolo was in a coma, Marian had a brief fling with old flame Jack Sugden.

The arrival on the scene of Tony Marchant, an NY Estates management trainee, caused friction between Jackie Merrick and Kathy Bates, who neverthe-less reassessed their on–off relationship and decided to get engaged. It was not the only time that Jackie fell in a big way: later in the year he had to be rescued from a mineshaft!

In the past, Matt had helped out an elderly recluse called Metcalfe on his farm, Crossgill, but was astonished to learn that he had been left the farm in the old man's will. Phoenix Developments was wound up, Phil Pearce going into partnership with ne'er-do-well Eric Pollard.

1988

Kathy and Jackie's relationship, turbulent at times, had a happy ending at St Mary's Church in February. Anxious for a place of their own, the couple settled at Demdyke in December.

It was a year of romances, some more

Dolly and Stephen Fuller's illicit relationship was to end in tragedy.

illicitly conducted than others. Springtime saw Jack Sugden and librarian Sarah Connolly stepping out for the first time, but Dolly's dalliance with timber consultant Stephen Fuller was not to be quite so public. They left on a secret holiday in June, but before the month was out Matt's wayward wife was confessing all to Annie.

Matt and Dolly had high hopes of moving to the renovated farmhouse at Crossgill, but its destruction by fire – Phil Pearce, the builder, had carelessly left rags to burn – put paid to that dream and nearly cost Annie her life. Fortunately, Pearce made partial amends by dashing into the blazing house to bring her to safety.

Crossgill was not the only residence to sustain damage this year: Archie Brooks's caravan was destroyed by Nick Bates in the Emmerdale tractor.

Nick had briefly been a hero in June when he foiled a robbery at Beckindale's post office, but tarnished his saint-

Archie's caravan is crushed by Nick on the Emmerdale tractor.

ly reputation somewhat by pocketing some of the discarded loot himself. However, he was not to enjoy his ill-gotten gains. He entrusted the money to girlfriend Clare Sutcliffe, who promptly went off to Leeds. Neither she nor the money was ever seen again. To add to his troubles, Eric Pollard and Phil Pearce learned of his crime and made life difficult for him for a while; but, that Christmas, he fingered Pollard and Pearce when they tried to steal antique fireplaces from Home Farm. Pearce confessed

Opposite: *Annie is rescued from Crossgill by Phil Pearce and Dolly Skilbeck.*

After a whirlwind courtship, Joe Sugden and Kate Hughes tie the knot at St Mary's Church.

all; but his business partner had, as ever, left no clues to his own involvement and remained beyond the reach of the law.

Alan Turner was also in trouble with the authorities: breathalysed and banned from driving for a year. His luck was out: a spell with a dating agency also failed to bring satisfaction.

However, love was blooming elsewhere in Beckindale, and as ever one of the Sugden brothers was involved.

Joe's interest in newly arrived divorcée Kate Hughes followed a series of unfortunate early meetings, in one of which he shot her dog for worrying sheep. In October he was the only person to turn up at her birthday party – uninvited – and the relationship soon blossomed. Kate came with responsibilities of her own, however, in teenage children Rachel and Mark.

Opposite: *Rachel and Mark Hughes, Kate's teenage tearaways.*

1989

Turning over a new leaf for a new year, Nick Bates finally confessed his part in the post office robbery in January – an eventful month, with Mark Hughes running away to Germany in an act of rebellion against his mother's new relationship with Joe (he only got as far as Hull) and Dolly leaving home on

Sgt MacArthur cautions Kate Sugden after her part in Pete Whiteley's death.

the final breakdown of her marriage to Matt. This was another problem for Annie as Emmerdale Farm matriarch; and it was apparent by now that her dependence on tranquillisers bordered on addiction.

Kate and Joe married in the parish church in April, the Reverend Donald Hinton relaxing his 'no divorcees' rule for the one and only occasion.

Sandie left for Scotland in May, opening the way for Eric Pollard to reclaim his old job as auctioneer at Hotten Market. Nick Bates resigned in disgust as Pollard's appointment was confirmed, and set off for France. Back home, his sister, Kathy, suffered a miscarriage after she contracted a disease of sheep, *Cryptosporidium*.

Alan Turner made two conquests in May, vanquishing Kate Sugden in a fight to sit on the district council and sweeping aside Mrs Bates's misgivings about their affair. Sadly, their plans of marriage proved unworkable, and she would leave in October for Scarborough. In another unexpected departure from the Beckindale scene, Matt Skilbeck left in November, unable to come to terms with the loss of wife Dolly. She, meanwhile, was briefly a kidnap victim when local farmer Ted Sharp misread her friendship as something quite different.

Two notable deaths this year were those of Jackie Merrick, who died in the summer when his own shotgun discharged while he was on the trail of a troublesome fox, and Dennis Rigg. Rigg's company had plans to turn the whole area into a quarry, and he was determined to acquire all the relevant properties – by fair means or foul. Having attempted to sabotage the efforts of Alan Turner and Joe Sugden at Home

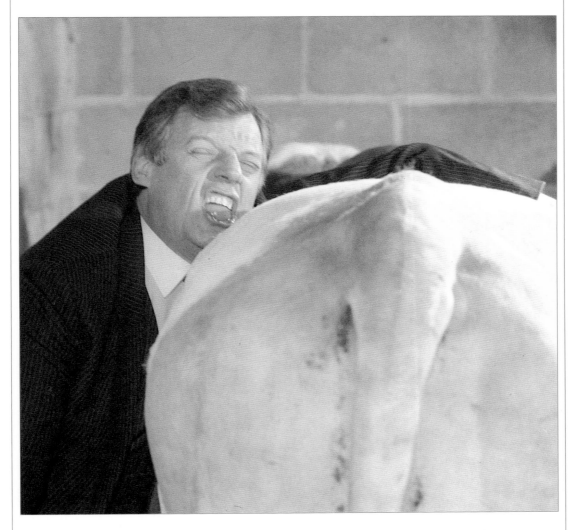

Dennis Rigg is crushed by Joe's bull, thus putting an end to his dubious expansion plans.

Farm, he turned his attention to Emmerdale. One night as he skulked around the outbuildings he was crushed by Joe's prize bull.

A peregrine falcon's nest found itself under threat from egg thieves. Jack Sugden and Henry Wilks kept watch at Keller Fell to ensure that the majestic birds of prey survived.

Finally, 1989 saw a change of ownership at Home Farm as Frank Tate, self-made haulage magnate, moved in with second wife Kim, son Chris (now running the family business), and daughter Zoë who was training to be a vet. Very soon Dolly had moved into a flat at Home Farm with son Sam when the Tates employed her as housekeeper.

SAW THIS

1990

A year that would turn out to be fated for Joe and Kate Sugden began with Joe being caught illegally putting steroid implants into his beef cattle. In May troublesome stepson Mark was caught shoplifting – an event followed swiftly by his mother losing Joe's baby. Kate's ex-husband, David Hughes, who had left the Army and returned to England in the hope of winning Kate back, sneaked into the milking-shed one morning and threatened Joe with a shotgun. Fortunately Kate arrived and managed to defuse the situation.

But worse was to follow in August when Kate accidentally ran down and killed Pete Whiteley, the man who had been having an affair with her daughter, in a road accident. She was sent to gaol for manslaughter in October, leaving Joe in charge of her two wayward teenagers.

Zoë Tate led a youth movement against hare-coursing, catching Jock McDonald red-handed. Pete Whiteley's widow, Lynne, gave birth to a son, Peter, on the day of her husband's funeral. Elsa Feldmann was also pregnant, but not from choice: her marriage to the father, Nick Bates, was swiftly scheduled, and both moved under mother Elizabeth Feldmann's roof – in separate beds!

Frank Tate, the recently installed owner of Home Farm, was making news, admitting publicly at the hunt ball that he had assisted the death of his terminally ill first wife, Jean, in 1984. He was under pressure from a former employee, George Starkey, who had discovered the truth of the matter and was blackmailing him. Five months after this dramatic confession, Frank hit the bottle and failed to attend daughter Zoe's graduation. Meanwhile, a barn conversion at Home Farm burned down, and arson was suspected. Since Tate had recently closed his mother's farm on economic grounds, Michael Feldmann was suspected and charged, but was later exonerated when

Jock MacDonald, hare-courser, fire-raiser and all-round petty criminal.

SAW PART OF 1990 THEN SHOW NOT ON, THEN STARTED AT KATE'S TRIAL

Jock MacDonald was found to be the fire-raiser.

The romance between Frank's son Chris and attractive young widow Kathy Merrick gathered pace after an April night of passion, and by early summer she was living at Home Farm.

Nick Bates and local layabout Archie Brooks had also found a new home, squatting in Demdyke.

Job cuts were hitting the Dales once more: the mobile library was axed, and with it Sarah Connolly's post. Jack volunteered her for bar work at the Woolpack – and, much to her surprise, she found herself enjoying it. Her help was more than welcome after Amos suffered a stroke during Annie's seventieth-birthday celebrations in July.

A year that began with Kathy finding Seth Armstrong unconscious in Dracula's coffin (a prop in the village play) ended with a chemical-tanker crash in the village: luckily, neither incident proved to have fatal consequences.

NOT SEEN

Fatalities are avoided when a chemical tanker crashed in Beckindale's main street.

1991

It was the end of an era at the Woolpack, Beckindale's social centre, when Amos Brearly called time on his thirty-two years as landlord to retire to Spain. The new landlord was to be former Home Farm boss Alan Turner, who immediately turned the tap room into a restaurant and sent the place up-market – only for a policewoman strip-pogram to lower the tone somewhat that August.

Times were hard at Tate Haulage, with the yard lease up for sale and Frank considering hijacking one of his own lorries for the insurance money. Elsewhere, corrupt councillor Charlie Aindow called in a £2,000 loan from Eric Pollard, forcing his auctioneer associate to sell his car to raise the cash.

Though Elsa and Nick's wedding day was arranged to coincide with St Valentine's Day, little else went to plan. An unexpected guest in the shape of baby Alice interrupted proceedings, and the wedding was delayed indefinitely. If that

Amos takes wing from the Woolpack in search of sunnier climes.

relationship was yet to be cemented, Joe and Kate Sugden's proved to be on shaky ground after she was released from prison. Finding it impossible to endure the inevitable wagging tongues and return to Beckindale, she ended the marriage in August. All was rosier for daughter Rachel, whose engagement to farmhand Michael Feld-mann was announced in June, and also for Chris Tate and Kathy Merrick, who tied the knot later in the year.

The wedding was accompanied by unscheduled drama when Sarah Connolly was kidnapped by Jim Latimer, recently released from prison. Jack Sugden had been his main accuser when he was convicted in 1973 of the murder of his girlfriend, Sharon Crosthwaite, and he was bent on revenge. Holding Jack's partner hostage in a disused building, he caused his adversary untold worry, though Sarah (who not only looked like Latimer's former girlfriend but also had the same

Alan Turner feels the long arm of the law as he takes over behind the Woolpack bar – though her undercover mission of birthday greetings soon becomes apparent.

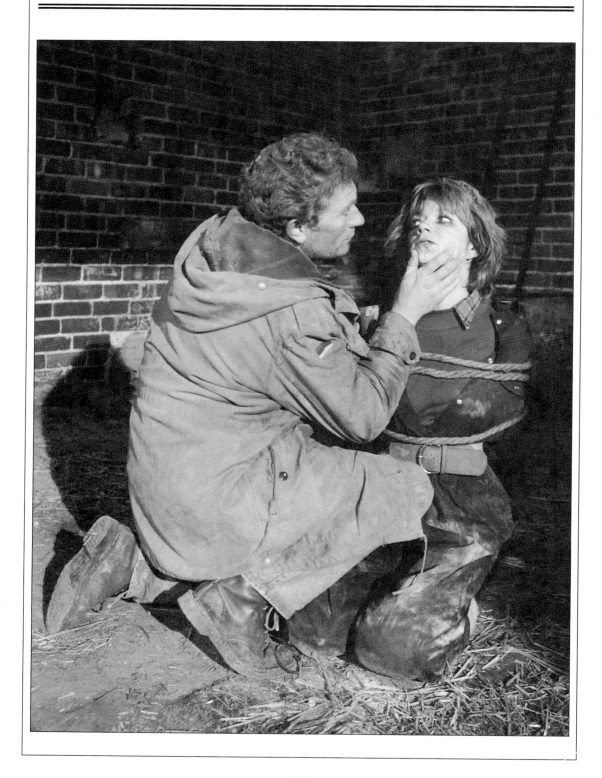

Opposite: *Jim Latimer, a man with scores to settle, holds Sarah Connolly captive.*

initials) was surprisingly sympathetic to his plight.

Direct action of a different kind had taken place earlier in the year when Michael, Archie and Zoë went on an Animal Rights raid in March: unfortunately for Zoë, the target was her place of work – a Hotten veterinary practice.

She left both her job and the area three months afterwards, selling Pollard her well-worn MG sports-car as she headed for her new job as a flying vet in New Zealand.

Dolly Skilbeck had a brief affair with Councillor Charlie Aindow; she became pregnant, had an abortion and departed for Norfolk with son Sam soon after. Beckindale also said goodbye in 1991 to the sadly departed Bill Whiteley and Henry Wilks.

Lynn Whiteley mourns the sudden loss of her two-timing husband Pete.

1992

Elsa having left him on Christmas Eve 1991, bound for the bright lights of Leeds and taking baby Alice with her, Nick Bates faced 1992 in understandably cheerless mood. The return of baby Alice to be raised by her father lifted the gloom somewhat, but posed a new set of problems. Holding down his job as Home Farm gardener and looking after his daughter would be a struggle – Nick's mother, Caroline, was so concerned that she returned from Scarborough to keep an eye on things. By that time, however, Archie Brooks had taken on the responsibility for Alice's welfare while Nick was at work, finally leaving his lodgings at Whiteley's farm to become Beckindale's most unlikely live-in nanny.

Nick had been busy at the holiday village, which opened its doors in early

Sixth former Melanie Clifford, the long-suffering girlfriend of Mark Hughes.
Opposite: *Single father Nick Bates feeds daughter Alice at their Demdyke home.*

summer. But owner Frank Tate's dream turned sour in June when wife Kim fell from her horse at the Hotten Show, breaking a leg and losing the baby they had tried so hard to create after Frank's vasectomy reversal. In Kim's absence, master-of-foxhounds Neil Kincaid arrived on the scene, eager – too eager perhaps? – to lend a hand at the stables.

The Woolpack had its share of excitement, too, on both sides of the bar. Seth's promotion to the credit-card class ended in penury when wife Meg purloined the plastic, while Carol Nelson was having trouble combining her barmaid's job with single parenthood. Teenage rebel Lorraine would clearly give her mother more grey hairs before the year was out.

Eric Pollard, Hotten Market auctioneer and bad guy, seemed to have changed his ways owing to the calming, not to say charming, influence of Elizabeth Feldmann. Their engagement brought opposition from her son, Michael, but Eric even seemed to be winning him round – just! They were married in September. Another troublesome son, Mark Hughes, was causing stepfather Joe Sugden headaches of a different kind, ducking his last A-level examination and renouncing a university career – a step that brought disapproval not only from Joe but also from Mark's girlfriend, Melanie Clifford who called him a wimp and ended their relationship.

'Emmerdale' Happiness and Heartaches

In the beginning, critics claimed that 'Emmerdale' was a sleepy slow-moving turn-off. Twenty years on, it is easy to see how wrong they were. Just as in real life, the inhabitants of Beckindale have known their share of happiness and heartache, and several events over the years have united the close-knit community in joy or in grief.

The series started on a note of heartbreak, of course, with the funeral of Jacob Sugden. Although he was never seen on screen, it is known that he was a drinker and had let the farm deteriorate in recent years. While his death was lamented, at the same time it opened a new chapter in Emmerdale Farm's long history by letting the next generation take on the responsibilities.

Farmhand Matt Skilbeck came to know heartbreak only too well in the early years of the series. Yet all was smiles when Peggy gave birth to twins Sam and Sarah (Sally) in February 1973. The family moved the short distance from Emmerdale to the

Opposite: The marriage of Janie Harker to Frank Blakey in March 1973 was the first 'Emmerdale' wedding to be screened. Joe Sugden and Christine Sharp followed in 1974.

farmhouse at Jamieson's, a smallholding of about thirty acres.

Only months later, however, Matt rushed into the Emmerdale farmhouse – Peggy wouldn't wake up. Her tragic death from a burst blood-vessel in the brain occurred when the twins were just three months old, and she was buried alongside her father in the village churchyard. The twins, meanwhile, went to live at Blackfell, some three miles away, with Matt's Aunt Beattie.

The first Beckindale wedding, between Janie Harker and village blacksmith Frank Blakey at St Mary's Parish Church, was seen in March 1973. Performing the ceremony was the Reverend Edward Ruskin, first in a line of Beckindale vicars.

Tragedy struck the Skilbecks yet again later in 1973 when Aunt Beattie's car stalled on a level crossing with the twins in the back. A train ploughed into it, with fatal results. A policeman stopped Matt's car to break the news, after which he spent the night away from the farmhouse, roaming the moors blind with grief and self-loathing. 'Why should I live when the rest of my family were dead?' he raged. 'What was the point?'

The year 1974 was memorable for the

*Silver Jubilee 1977. The outdoor party held in Beckindale was
a great success thanks to the very fine weather.*

marriage of Joe and glamorous milk-recorder Christine Sharp. Henry Wilks gave the bride away since her father did not consider her ready for such a big step. (He was right: she could not adjust to farm life and, though a reconciliation was attempted, the couple divorced.) But the great day was enjoyed by all, with the men resplendent in morning suits, Annie all smiles and Matt as best man.

In 1977 communities all over the country were unravelling the red, white and blue bunting unused since the Coronation to celebrate the Silver Jubilee of Her Majesty Queen Elizabeth II; and, though Beckindale has few streets, its street-party was indeed a sight to behold. 'What a spread we put on that day,' said a satisfied Annie. Children with painted faces ran amok as Joe Sugden, resplendent in purple top-hat, helped Henry Wilks and Amos Brearly to organise things from the head of a very long trestle-table.

Happiness there was a-plenty when Jack Sugden and Pat Merrick rediscovered each other. The former Pat Harker had enjoyed a teenage romance with Jack, which ended before the headstrong youth realised that he had made her pregnant. When Pat married Tom Merrick on the rebound, everyone naturally assumed that Jackie was *his* son – and when the truth got out the lad was understandably resentful of the father he had never known who had run away from his responsibilities. This very public rebellion did not stop Jack and Pat from marrying at Hotten register office in 1982, though Jack and Tom Merrick (who still loved his ex-wife despite beating her and causing

Jack Sugden marries Pat witnessed by Sam Pearson, Annie, Matt Skilbeck, Jackie Merrick and Joe.

her to leave him) had settled their differences with a brawl outside the Woolpack.

The couple's happiness continued with the birth of their son Robert in early 1986. But heartache was soon to follow in August when Pat died in an accident. As she swerved to avoid a flock of sheep, her car plunged down a hillside, with fatal results. Since the couple had not long been reconciled after his affair with auctioneer's assistant Karen Moore, the blow to Jack was particularly hard.

Now married, Matt and Dolly Skilbeck had been enduring heartaches after the happy birth of son Sam in 1982. After the double strain of the return of Dolly's illegitimate son and Matt's arrest for the murder of Harry Mowlem, the couple sought to rebuild their lives at Crossgill, an old farmhouse bequeathed to them by a local eccentric. But it was not to be: the old farmhouse burned down in 1988, with Phil Pearce – whose carelessness had caused the fire in the first place – preventing further heartbreak by rescuing Annie, who was trapped inside.

Dolly responded to this setback by running into the arms not of Matt but of forestry consultant Stephen Fuller. Though she wouldn't run away to live with him as he asked, he offered excitement Matt could never hope to equal, and Dolly found it hard to resist his charms. On the day she finally broke off the relationship after Stephen had reappeared in Kelthwaite, he was killed by a falling tree. Feeling responsible, Dolly took charge of his funeral, which Matt attended in the vain hope of regaining her affections. At Christmas the marriage finally broke down, and Dolly moved out of the house with Sam.

That was not the end of Dolly's misfortunes. The following year, 1989, she was kidnapped by Ted Sharp, a local farmer whom she had befriended. Having cleaned his house, made him a birthday cake and taken Sam for tea, she found her actions interpreted in a less than innocent way, and was imprisoned in a bedroom for forty-eight hours as he tried to persuade her to stay. A subsequent ill-advised affair with councillor Charlie Aindow led to an abortion, and she left the area soon after.

Kathy Bates and Jackie Merrick enjoyed a long courtship with more than its share of ups and downs – one of the latter being an incident in which Jackie smashed up the van of Tony Marchant, a rival for Kathy's affections during a break in their relationship. Their marriage in February 1988 was equally eventful: a burst water-tank at the Bateses' cottage ruined Kathy's wedding dress overnight, but Annie saved the day by offering her own Edwardian dress as a replacement. The surprise news that the couple were expecting a baby in the spring of 1989 brought much happiness to the respective families. As it transpired, Kathy miscarried after she had contracted the sheep disease *Cryptosporidium*, but that was far from the only heartache the year was to bring.

Jackie Merrick lost his life in the summer of 1989, all for the sake of a £10 bet. A fox that had terrorised Alan Turner's game became Public Enemy Number One when it turned its attention to local smallholders' poultry. Seth decided to dig it out, but Jackie was convinced he could shoot it. The wager was struck, and Jackie kept a vigil which extended after darkness.

Jackie arrived in his Land-Rover just as the fox was leaving his den and picked it out clearly in the headlights. As he opened the door and reached into the car for the shotgun, still keeping a steady eye on the fox, the trigger snagged and Jackie fell to the ground by the Land-Rover with the engine still running, the lights still on and the radio playing.

Meanwhile, Kathy and Lynn Whiteley waited, with Kathy growing more and more anxious. When Jackie had still not returned next morning, Seth Armstrong set off to the fox's den to discover Jackie's body – still lying where he had fallen. Later that day, Kathy, clutching at Joe Sugden for support, and in the presence of Sergeant MacArthur, formally identified the body of John Jacob Merrick.

Recently arrived in Hotten from Sheffield, Kate Hughes met Joe in 1988, but it had hardly been love at first sight: they argued first in a restaurant, then in a supermarket. He shot her dog, which had been worrying sheep, an unlikely relationship developed and they were married at St Mary's in April 1989, the Reverend Donald Hinton relaxing his 'no divorcees' rule for the first and last time.

Though it started with the news that they were expectant parents, 1990 was a particularly tragic year for Joe and Kate Sugden. A miscarriage in May followed Kate's son Mark's arrest for shoplifting. Her daughter, Rachel, meanwhile, was involved with a married man, Pete Whiteley. Then, in August, Kate killed Whiteley, who had returned from Birmingham where he had gone once his affair with Rachel had been discovered, in a road accident. A breathalyser test proved positive, and a prison sentence followed.

When Kate was released from prison

Rachel Hughes, still a schoolgirl, soon caught the eye of married salesman Pete Whiteley.

in 1991 she was scarred and shocked by prison life. She could not accept the attitude of Joe and the family, who bent over backwards to help her, and she also encountered some understandable hostility in the village – especially from Pete's widow, Lynn, and his grandfather. Kate left for 'a break' with her father, but she found that she could not resume her old life and departed for good, her children remaining under Emmerdale's roof in Joe's care.

Kathy Merrick and Christopher Tate had a stormy courtship but, when they finally married in November 1991, Kathy said it was the happiest day of her life. Chris had made every attempt to see Kathy on the morning of the wedding,

With typical Tate razzmatazz, Frank organised a helicopter trip to the wedding reception.

but Caroline Bates kept him at bay as tradition demanded, then asked her ex-husband, Malcolm, to drive the bride round the block a few times to make Chris sweat a bit! They ran into a traffic jam, which made them late, and the bride ended up racing down Hotten High Street to the register office.

Father Frank Tate, who had been denied his wish to give them a lavish wedding, took some pleasure from the fact that his small reception turned out to be a massive affair after Kathy and Christopher had been whisked from the ceremony to Home Farm by helicopter – another surprise arranged by Dad.

To cap the evening, as the newlyweds prepared to leave for their honeymoon, Frank accompanied them to the front door where they were treated to a spectacular firework display, concluding with a giant burning heart enclosing the names Kathy and Chris.

As so often happens in 'Emmerdale', the happiness of the wedding was followed by potential heartbreak: the mysterious disappearance of Sarah Connolly, kidnapped by Jim Latimer, recently released after a prison sentence for a murder for which Jack had helped to convict him in 1973. But disaster was avoided.

Two decades of happiness and heartache in 'Emmerdale' have made for riveting viewing. Who knows what the coming years will bring?

They Also Served

Now that the main centres in and around Beckindale have more or less been established as Emmerdale Farm, Home Farm, the Holiday Village and the Woolpack, it is interesting to recall the other locations, businesses and tradespeople that have featured since 1972.

It's an oddity of Beckindale that the village shop is almost never seen except as a meeting-point in the street or as a convenient location for a chat while waiting for the bus.

The first shop seen by the viewers was run by Amy Postleton, who was, in 1974, handing over to Norah Norris. For a short time, until 1975, the shop interior appeared as a regular location. The most recent incumbent is Mrs Robson.

Sgt MacArthur's right hand man notifies Dolly Skilbeck of the death of her lover, Stephen Fuller.

Dr Clare Scott, who spent five years in Beckindale before leaving in 1977.

Ruth Pennington assisted Mr Braithwaite, the vet, and nearly married Joe Sugden.

The village shop also serves as a post office, but the mail has been delivered first by Barney and latterly by Tom. Their surnames are not known, but Beckindale is that sort of community.

The long arm of the law is seldom called into action, but in recent years Kate's misdemeanour, the arson attack at Home Farm, the kidnapping of Sarah and the crushing to death of Dennis Rigg by Joe Sugden's prize bull must have kept the notebooks and pencils busy.

Ted Edwards policed Beckindale from 1977 to 1980. Since then Sergeant MacArthur from Hotten police station has been on hand to cover all breaches of the peace. Nowadays he is sometimes accompanied by PC Davies.

The health of the community has been entrusted to four GPs since 1972 when Dr Grant retired to be replaced by

Dr Clare Scott. In 1977, Dr Jacobs took over the practice, but he retired in 1985 when Dr Sharma – whose daughter, Sita, was Jackie Merrick's girlfriend – took over.

An important role in the community is naturally the vet, and the first vet seen about Emmerdale was John Stokes from 1980–2. John Stokes took on a young apprentice called Martin Butler in 1982. At the same time a new female vet, Margaret Beckett, was also practising.

In 1987 attractive Ruth Pennington came to work for Mr Braithwaite, who then ran the practice, and soon was romantically involved with Joe Sugden. When things did not work out with Joe, she left.

When Zoë Tate graduated, she was employed by Martin Bennett as his assistant, but left in 1991 appalled at his involvement with animal experimentation for Skipdale Laboratories.

Goodwin's practice is also used by Emmerdale Farm.

The livestock from Emmerdale Farm and its neighbours inevitably end up in the auction-pens at Hotten Market where they frequently also offer the land and movables from the big local estates that come under the hammer.

Hotten Market is currently run by the

Having quit Bennett's veterinary surgery in disgust at their animal experimentation, Zoë Tate left Beckindale for New Zealand with a middle-aged lover in tow.

council, but was once owned by Arthur Golding. His family had owned the market for three generations. Owing to ill health Golding had to sell out to Joe Sugden's NY Estates in 1986. The Market was sold for demolition in 1987, but reopened in 1988 under the control of the council.

The first auctioneer seen at Hotten Market was James Price in 1978 when he handled the sale of the Verney Estate; his assistant was Judy Westrop. Then came Karen Moore in 1984 with Sandie Merrick as her assistant. Sandie took over after Eric Pollard, Karen's successor, was sacked by Joe Sugden for dishonesty.

When Sandie left for Scotland in 1989, Eric Pollard – no doubt because of his connection with councillor Charlie Aindow – was reinstated.

Very much tied up with the market these days is the parish council, which in its time has included in its number Henry Wilks. Today Alan Turner and Charlie Aindow are concerned with council affairs, even if slightly at odds in their motivation.

Beckindale parish church was founded in AD 989, and births, marriages and deaths have always called for the presence of a vicar in the series. By far the best-known and longest-serving was the Reverend Donald Hinton, who stayed in Beckindale for twelve years, from 1977 to 1989. During his absences over those years, his locum was usually the Reverend Bob Jerome. In 1982, Donald Hinton's assistant minister was briefly the Reverend Bill Jeffries, who relinquished the position because of their differing views.

The most recent minister was Tony Charlton, who left in 1991 after involving himself in much local activity and

regularly visiting Kate Sugden in prison, but falling in love with Kathy Merrick in the process. He left Beckindale for London when he realised Kathy was still in love with Christopher Tate.

Since then we have seen one fleeting appearance by the Reverend Jackson, who is helping out till a permanent minister takes up the position.

Lastly, a very important service is provided by Ernie Shuttleworth, who runs the Malt Shovel. The beer is not up to the standard of the Woolpack, and the service is grudging; but, from time to time, the Malt Shovel is brought into the spotlight when troubles at the Woolpack send the drinkers elsewhere.

The Reverend David Cowper, the successor to William Hockley in Beckindale in 1977.

❖ L A N D M A R K S ❖

LITTLEWELL

LITTLEWELL is a small hamlet eight miles north-east of Hotten on the Beckindale road and is best-known for its nature reserve which houses a great number of endangered species of the plant and bird variety. Lacking church, shop or public house, most inhabitants look to the neighbouring town or village for their spiritual or worldly needs.

'Emmerdale' Then and Now

In its two screen decades 'Emmerdale' has moved on apace. Today's producer, Morag Bain, is keen that the stories reflect life in the north of England in the nineties.

From early-seventies beginnings of low-key dramas strictly within the rural setting of the series, today sees the people in and around Beckindale immersed in a totally different world – and one that often extends far beyond the parish boundaries. Range Rovers, mobile telephones and fax machines are now almost as plentiful as the trees, tractors and telegrams of yesteryear.

As society's views have changed, so inevitably have those of 'Emmerdale'. The series now has a single parent – and a male one at that – in Nick Bates. Although it is a struggle to balance his responsibilities, assisted by today's enlightened attitudes, he would surely have found his task well-nigh impossible in 1972 when the series started.

When divorcees Joe Sugden and Kathy Gimbel set up home in Demdyke in 1977, there was a public outcry. But Jack and Sarah, living together out of wedlock under the same roof as Annie, with Rachel Hughes and Michael Feldmann next door, scarcely raised an eyebrow in 1991. Rachel's earlier affair with married Pete Whiteley would have been another scandalous situation in 1972. Even Pete's wife, Lynn, overcame her initial resentment towards the young cuckoo in her nest and life went on – in sharp contrast to Dolly Skilbeck's anguish over her affair with timber specialist Stephen Fuller just two years earlier.

The sanctity of marriage in Beckindale is not all it once was. When Kate Sugden sailed out of Joe's life in a taxi, she felt no obligation to the man who had stood by her before, during and after her prison sentence for the manslaughter of Pete Whiteley. This was yet another sign of the times, with a Beckindale lady of property – and a *Sugden* at that – going through the agonies of a convicted felon.

The Tate family is the symbol of the new Beckindale. While Jack Sugden may rant and rave about townies taking over the countryside, there can be no doubting the impact that wealthy Frank, his glamorous wife and go-getter children have made on the locals. Son Christopher transformed the life of country girl Kathy, now buying expensive outfits in Harrogate and recording pop songs composed by Christopher, when once she was satisfied with yesterday's fashions and a husband whose idea of a good time was a pint or three in the Woolpack.

Regulars at that hostelry in the seventies would be amazed, if not shocked, to see the new rustic 'theme' décor and Alan Turner, in the guise of master chef, serving up Cordon Bleu meals in his restaurant in the old taproom.

Talk in the Woolpack now veers towards vintage wine and *filet mignon* rather than the more traditional topics of

slurry, lambing and dominoes. Why, even Seth Armstrong, the archetypal bar-propping regular of Amos Brearly's day, has now become the owner of a credit card.

Eric Pollard – to some an entrepreneur, to others a crook – could certainly not have survived the seventies, while his one-time partner Charlie Aindow typifies the opportunist who, if the press are to be believed, sits on many modern-day councils.

Things have certainly changed in Beckindale. But what of the future? Will Rachel's university position lead to new

Kathy and Christopher Tate: she married into wealth and the high life but took some time to acclimatise to Christopher's overbearing ways.

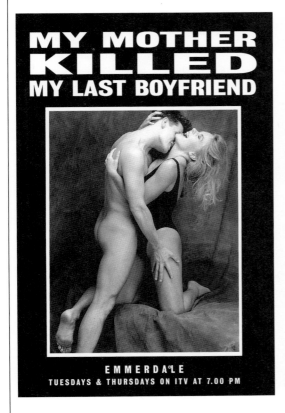

Rachel Hughes called off her wedding plans with Michael Feldmann because she found him boring. These Yorkshire Television press advertisements, published during 1992 to attract younger viewers, suggest Michael was anything but boring

avenues in the big city? Will Annie's wanderlust, which sees her swanning off to Spain and Glyndebourne, herald the break-up of the Sugden family? Will Frank Tate graduate from the holiday village to a ten-pin bowling alley or a theme park? Will Seth get a mobile telephone?

Only the producers and the story-writers know the answers. Whatever they decide, we may be sure that 'Emmerdale' will still be entertaining us into the twenty-first century and the characters and situations will be as real and as sympathetic to the times as they are today.

EMMERDALE FARM

EMMERDALE FARM, twenty years on, is still the focal point of the series. The house is over ten times older than the show itself, and stands on the site of a similar building that pre-dated it. The current farm incorporates walls of its predecessor, just as the outbuildings and barns have been successively modified and updated over the centuries.

The farm covers about 300 acres, which are used to rear hens, geese, cattle (for beef and for milk) and sheep. There is also common grazing land on Pencross Fell, which has been shared with Home Farm in the past. Seventy acres were added to Emmerdale land in 1987 with the addition of Crossgill, which Matt and Dolly Skilbeck inherited from a recluse called Metcalfe. The land would not have been viable as a separate farm, so they sold the land to renovate the farmhouse – which burned down.

As well as the accredited herd of Friesian cows, there are about 700 sheep – 450 Mashams and 250 Swaledales. Lambing is at the end of March. There is a farm shop which was built by Dolly and Kathy in the summer of 1988 to sell eggs, poultry, cheese and milk.

The Sugden family acquired a leasehold interest in Emmerdale in the nineteenth century when Josh Sugden sacrificed his life in the Crimean War saving the son of Yorkshire landowner Lord Miffield. Josh's wife and son inherited the lease as a mark of gratitude. Only barley crops for malting were raised until 1901 when Paul Sugden, Josh's grandson, purchased a herd of dairy cattle after a run of very poor harvests. An outbreak of foot and mouth disease the following year failed to weaken his resolve, and so it is that Emmerdale has an accredited herd today.

The Sugdens always assumed that their tenure at Emmerdale was unlimited, not realising that the freehold could possibly be obtained from the Miffield estate by a third party. That, of course, is what Henry Wilks did, and Emmerdale Farm Ltd came into existence shortly afterwards – a change which has undoubtedly been to the farm's benefit.

The building itself has at least two storeys, and is connected to the two-bedroom annexe that was once occupied by the Skilbecks. Jack moved in on Christmas Day 1989. Sarah nailed the connecting door up shortly after moving in with Jack, to avoid any unannounced visits by Annie; but it was opened again in early 1992 during a lingerie party – with amusing results.

Cast List

PHYLLIS ACASTER
Jean Heywood

CHARLIE AINDOW
David Fleeshman

ALEX
Guy Scantlebury

RICHARD ANSTEY
Carl Rigg

MEG ARMSTRONG
Ursula Camm/Ruth Holden

SETH ARMSTRONG
Stan Richards

GEOFF ATWILL
Anthony Carrick

ALICE BATES (*grandmother*)
Olivia Jardith

ALICE BATES (*baby*)
Kimberley Hewitt

CAROLINE BATES
Diana Davies

KATHY BATES
Malandra Burrows

MALCOLM BATES
Tom Adams

NICK BATES
Cy Chadwick

MARGARET BECKETT
Susan Wooldridge

MARTIN BENNETT
John Pickles

FRANK BLAKEY
Eric Allan

ARTHUR BRAITHWAITE
Max Wall

AMOS BREARLY
Ronald Magill

EMILY BREARLY
Ann Way

ARCHIE BROOKS
Tony Pitts

MARTIN BUTLER
Steve Morley

ALISON CASWELL
Julie Brennan

THE REVEREND TONY CHARLTON
Stephen Rashbrook

MELANIE CLIFFORD
Joanne Woodcock

SARAH CONNOLLY
Madeleine Howard

PIP COULTER
Julie Dawn Cole

THE REVEREND DAVID COWPER
John Abbot

DAN
Julian Walsh

MAJOR DENYER
Kevin Storey

PC TED EDWARDS
Barry Hart

ELIZABETH FELDMANN
Kate Dove

ELSA FELDMANN
Naomi Lewis

From left to right;
BACK ROW: *Richard Thorp, Philomena McDonagh;*
THIRD ROW: *Peter Amory, Norman Bowler, Tony Pitts, Christopher Chittell, Matthew Vaughan, Stan Richards;*
SECOND ROW: *Malandra Burrows, Claire King, Cy Chadwick holding Kimberley Hewitt, Fionnuala Ellwood holding Sam Walker, Kate Dove, Craig McKay;*
FRONT ROW: *Madeleine Howard, Christopher Smith, Clive Hornby (behind), Diana Davies, Sheila Mercier, Frazer Hines, Glenda McKay.*

MICHAEL FELDMANN
Matthew Vaughan

PHIL FLETCHER
Kenneth Watson

TERRY FLETCHER
Bernard Padden

STEPHEN FULLER
Gregory Floy

GARY
Gary Halliday

LESLEY GIBSON
Jane Collins

FREDA GIMBEL
Mary Henry

JIM GIMBEL
John Atkinson

KATHY GIMBEL
Polly Hemmingway

MARTIN GIMBEL
George Fenton

DR GRANT
Arthur Hewlett

ASTA GUNNARSON
Madeline Hinde

OLOF GUNNARSON
Jurgen Anderson

JANIE HARKER
Diane Grayson

SYD HARKER
Andrew Bradford

ED HATHERSAGE
Paul Maxwell

STEVE HAWKER
Paul Rosebury

DANIEL HAWKINS
Alan Starkey

CLIVE HINTON
Martin Potter

THE REVEREND DONALD HINTON
Hugh Manning

THE REVEREND WILLIAM HOCKLEY
Jonathan Newth

DRYDEN HOGBEN
Roy Boyd

DAVID HUGHES
Martin Whitby

KATE HUGHES
Sally Knyvette

MARK HUGHES
Craig McKay

RACHEL HUGHES
Glenda McKay

DR JACOBS
Alick Hayes

JAN
Alison Dowling

THE REVEREND BILL JEFFRIES
James Aubrey

THE REVEREND BOB JEROME
Richard Howard

JEAN KENDALL
Lesley Nunnerly

ROSEMARY KENDALL
Lesley Manville

THE HON. NEIL KINCAID
Brian Deacon

JIM LATIMER
Miles Reitherman/Dennis Blanch

VIRGINIA LATTIMORE
Wanda Moore

LISA
Bryonie Pritchard

GRAHAM LODSWORTH
Ross Kemp

ANDY LONGTHORN
Mark Botham

SERGEANT IAN MacARTHUR
Martin Dale

JOCK MacDONALD
Drew Dawson

LIZ MacDONALD
Elizabeth Mickery

IRENE MADDEN
Kathleen Byron

MAGGIE
Jacqueline Redding

TONY MARCHANT
Mark Payton

CHRISTOPHER MEADOWS
Conrad Phillips

JACKIE MERRICK
Ian Sharrock

SANDIE MERRICK
Jane Hutcheson

TOM MERRICK
Edward Peel/Jack Carr

METCALFE
Bernard Kay

BILL MIDDLETON
Johnny Caesar

ANTHONY MOEKETSI
Oscar James

KAREN MOORE
Annie Hulley

HARRY MOWLEM
Godfrey James

CAROL NELSON
Philomena McDonagh

LORRAINE NELSON
Nicola Strong

NORAH NORRIS
Barbara Ashcroft

LESLEY PEARCE
Clare Clifford

PHIL PEARCE
Peter Alexander

SAM PEARSON
Toke Townley

RUTH PENNINGTON
Julia Chambers

BARBARA PETERS
Rosie Kerslake

BRIAN PETERS
Roger Davidson

ERIC POLLARD
Christopher Chittell

AMY POSTLETON
Dorothy Frere

ANGELA READ
Joanne Whalley

ANGIE RICHARDS
Beverley Callard

DENNIS RIGG
Richard Franklin

RICHARD ROPER
David Horovitch

PAOLO ROSSETTI
Carl Forgione

THE REVEREND EDWARD RUSKIN
George Little

DR SHARMA
Rashid Karapiet

SITA SHARMA
Mamta Kash

CHRISTINE SHARP Angela Cheyne	**CHRISTOPHER TATE** Peter Amory
ROBERT SHARP Bernard Kay	**FRANK TATE** Norman Bowler
TED SHARP Andy Rashleigh	**KIM TATE** Claire King
DOREEN SHUTTLEWORTH Sandra Gough	**ZOE TATE** Leah Bracknell
ERNIE SHUTTLEWORTH John Comer/Peter Schofield	**TREVOR THATCHER** Michael Cadman
DOLLY SKILBECK Katherine Barker/Jean Rogers	**JANET THOMPSON** Muriel Pavlow
MATT SKILBECK Frederick Pyne	**ENOCH TOLLY** Neil McCarthy
PEGGY SKILBECK Jo Kendall	**GRACE TOLLY** Margaret Stallard
SAM SKILBECK Benjamin Whitehead	**ALAN TURNER** Richard Thorp
GEORGE STARKEY James Noble	**JILL TURNER** Patricia Maynard
JOHN STOKES Stephen Malatratt	**TERENCE TURNER** Stephen Marchant
LUCY STUBBS Adrienne Frank	**CHARLOTTE VERNEY** Angela Thorne
ANNIE SUGDEN Sheila Mercier	**GEORGE VERNEY** Patrick Holt
JACK SUGDEN Andrew Burt/Clive Hornby	**GERALD VERNEY** James Kerry
JOE SUGDEN Frazer Hines	**DEREK WARNER** Freddie Fletcher
PAT SUGDEN Helen Weir	**BRUCE WESTROP** James Cossins
ROBERT SUGDEN Christopher Smith	**MAURICE WESTROP** Edward Dentith
CLARE SUTCLIFFE Sara Griffiths	**BILL WHITELEY** Teddy Turner

CAST LIST

LYNN WHITELEY
Fionnuala Ellwood

PETE WHITELEY
Jim Millea

PETE WHITELEY JR
Sam Walker

ALICE WILKS
Hazel Bainbridge

HENRY WILKS
Arthur Pentelow

MARIAN WILKS
Debbie Blyth

DEBBIE WILSON
Debbie Arnold